EXPERIENCES OF A PARANORMAL INVESTIGATOR

by

KIERAN WOODHOUSE

Contents

__Introduction__

Having a paranormal experience can be life changing. For a person who does not believe in the spirit world, experiencing something that they cannot explain, whether that be a touch on the shoulder, a disembodied voice calling out or a memorable spirit board session, it could alter their belief system entirely and make them question everything from that moment on. On the other hand, for a believer, experiencing any paranormal phenomena can simply solidify their own beliefs, making them as sure as they ever were that spirits do indeed exist and that they can interact with what we believe to be our physical world.

It is no secret that a person has to be open to experiencing the paranormal in order to get the best out of investigating the spirit world. If you set out on an investigation to prove that ghosts do exist, and with the mindset that you will always find evidence with a certainty, then you categorically will. Every shadow that you see will be a ghost. Every noise that you hear will be a spirit attempting to contact you. If you are feeling a little strange, maybe you have a headache or you feel a little nauseous, then it can be accredited to a paranormal experience. No further explanation will be needed for you. To put it simply, it was a ghost and there is no need to try and explain any occurrence logically because the activity is proving that your beliefs are right. However, if you enter an investigation with absolute certainty that ghosts do not exist and that you will encounter absolutely nothing at all, then nine times out of ten that will also be the case. With this mindset, every shadow that you see will always be able to be explained away. Every noise that you hear can also be explained. One of the problems with this approach, though, is that you can be too closed minded, pushing aside any evidence that is found, sometimes even if your explanation does not quite fit with what has actually happened.

Since becoming a paranormal investigator, I have found that the best approach is to be somewhere in the middle of the two extreme examples that I have described above. In fact, I always set out on an investigation to disprove spirit activity. I understand that this may sound like the second example above; the non-believer approach, but it is a little different. I have had many experiences whilst investigating the paranormal, of which some will be described in detail throughout this book. However, I have found that the best approach is to investigate with the mindset of disproving spirits because only then will you adopt a logical explanation for certain occurrences, where there is no paranormal activity occurring. Where this mindset and approach differs from that of a complete non-believer is that you must approach the field with an open mind and understand that if something cannot be explained, and sometimes this is most certainly the case, then you have to be open to the possibility that it was actually a paranormal experience, and not simply be brushed to one side and dismissed without further investigation.

The issue with entering an investigation either as a firm non-believer or as an avid believer, is that both sets of people can often fall into the trap of experiencing something but not questioning it or trying to explain what has happened any further. If you are a non-believer, then, for you, spirits do not exist, so that particular experience cannot be paranormal and that is the end of the debate. No need to listen to any other possibility. Similarly, if you fall into the avid believer category, then what you experience is always going to be a spirit, so there is no need for you to investigate any further. However, it is important to remember that the key word throughout this is "investigate". To investigate, we must explore experiences and occurrences, taking them further than face value and consider all of the possibilities, whether that falls into your belief system or not. Simply ignoring evidence, or taking an experience at face value, is not investigating and will not help to further the field of paranormal investigation as a whole, as well as your own research. Sometimes, we must be prepared to step outside of our comfort zone into other areas that may make us feel uncomfortable, whether that be a non-believer being prepared to accept potential paranormal experiences, or a believer accepting that an occurrence may have been something natural and not paranormal at all. This is something we must all have in mind when we step out to investigate the spirit world.

My previous book, An Introduction to Paranormal Investigation, was written with the purpose of explaining to the reader how paranormal investigations are really conducted when compared to what I have now termed the "Entertainment Industry" type investigations that you see on television. I also wanted to explain what equipment might be used, along with how and why it is used and trying to give people an overall better understanding of investigation techniques, should they ever wish to go out and begin conducting their own research and investigations in to the paranormal. When beginning to think about the topic of my next book, I felt that the natural progression should be to write about the common experiences that people tend to encounter when on a paranormal investigation and when using the equipment that I detailed in my previous book. As always, when detailing throughout this book the encounters that myself and my fellow investigators have had, I will be looking at it with a sceptical eye. This does not mean that I fall into the firm non-believer camp, but that I like to consider all of the possibilities that may have led to, or may have caused, the experience, whether that be paranormal or not.

It is also important to add here that the experiences that I will be detailing are personal to the experiencer and is as accurately told as possible. The reason I mention this is because paranormal investigating is a very personal experience in itself. We can use as much equipment as we want to in order to aid in our research, but we need to understand that most equipment has the ability to be faulty, or that it can be affected by outside sources, such as mobile phones or other electrical equipment. With that in mind, one of the best pieces of "equipment" that we can use, in my opinion, is the human body. When someone experiences a touch, hears a voice, or sees some form of manifestation, then they know whether they can trust themselves in what they have experienced. If someone should feel the need to elaborate on an experience, or to create one that did not actually happen, then only they know that and they must live with the knowledge that it never truly happened. Equally, if someone does experience something, and they know that what they have seen, heard, or felt is as real as can be, then they know that they can trust their experience. To give an example of this, I have often been on an investigation and have been stood, or sat, next to another investigator who is absolutely adamant that they are seeing a shadow figure, or that they can hear footsteps or voices. Even though I am right next to this person, there have been times where I cannot, as much as I want to, see or hear what they are describing to me. This has also happened the other way around, where it was me that was experiencing something but seemed to be the only one in the room who was. This does not mean that the experiencer here is lying or is not truly experiencing what it is that they are describing. What it does mean is that they are having an extremely personal experience and it should be treated with respect and investigated further to try and help understand what it could have been that they have witnessed.

For those that have read my previous book, attended one of my presentations or listened to my podcasts, you will know of my thoughts when it comes to how spirits operate in this world and where they could be existing. In my opinion, it is all about frequencies and visible light. We see roughly, give or take, 0.05% of the light spectrum, what we call visible light, leaving a huge 99.95% of the light spectrum unseen to the human eye. I believe that it is in these unseen spectrums that spirits, entities, and energies are operating. Not only these, but other paranormal phenomena such as cryptids or aliens. I believe that we are all operating within the same "world" but vibrating on completely different frequencies altogether, which can prevent us from interacting with each other on a daily basis. For a more detailed description of this theory, please refer to my previous book, An Introduction to Paranormal Investigation, where I go into more detail about this and give some good analogies to help explain it a little further.

If you have read my previous book, it may be that it kickstarted you in to going out and investigating the paranormal for yourself. If that is the case, then hopefully by now your journey has given you some experiences of your own which can be likened to those that you are about to read. You may have noticed that the experiences that you are having are never quite the same and that they are all unique. To explain these experiences as easily as possible I will be breaking them down into categories, such as audible or visual, for example.

If you are a seasoned investigator, then I have no doubt that you will have had very similar experiences yourself and maybe this book can help you understand in more detail what it was that you have previously experienced.

Category One: Audible Experiences

An audible experience is no doubt one of the most commonly reported experiences when it comes to the reporting of paranormal activity. With that being said, I would go as far to say that a large percentage of audible experiences do not actually occur when on an investigation. I have heard of so many cases where people will be watching television in the comfort of their own home when, all of a sudden, they hear footsteps or knocking, and they cannot explain who, or what, is responsible for the noises.

When it comes to actually being on a paranormal investigation, the majority of attendees will have brought with them some type of device that enables them to hear their surroundings much clearer, or a device that can record the audio of the investigation, known by most as an EVP recorder. EVP – Electronic Voice Phenomena – recorders are a common tool in an investigator's kitbag and can aid greatly in finding evidence when out investigating.

As discussed in my previous book, the one thing that I find most interesting when it comes to EVP recorders is their ability to potentially record sounds that can fall outside of the human hearing range. Even if the person that is investigating has the widest possible hearing range for a human and prides themselves on how good their hearing is, it is still limited to what the human body can process. To test this, use a frequency emitter, or download one on your smart phone, and go through the full range of frequencies that are available. You will soon discover that there are sounds that cannot be heard by the human ear. The best example of this in action would be a dog whistle. The point that I am trying to make here is just because we cannot hear a sound, it does not mean that the noise is not happening.

If you were to take two people and play to them the range of frequencies through a frequency emitter you would see that the hearing range of everyone is completely different. One person will signal that they can no longer hear what is being emitted, yet the person standing right next to them, listening to the same device, will signal that they can still hear the frequencies being played. It is examples like this that can make investigating the paranormal so interesting, yet at the same time so frustrating. For those reading this who are seasoned investigators, you will understand what I mean when I say that someone in your group will be adamant that they can hear a particular noise, whether that be footsteps, voices, knocks and so on, yet maybe yourself or another group member will be certain that there are no noises occurring whatsoever. So, who is right? The simple answer is that both are right. Unless the person experiencing the noises is lying, which, don't get me wrong, can certainly be the case, then the noises are happening for them within the perception of their own reality. Just because the person next to them cannot hear the noises, that does not make them any less real.

With this in mind, try to imagine just how many noises are occurring around you on a daily basis that you cannot hear. Now, I am not saying that every noise you are missing out on is paranormal, of course. What I am saying is that when you are investigating, try to understand that the human body is limited to what it can experience. Using tools, such as EVP recorders, will very much help you to capture some of those sounds that you may have otherwise missed, but there will be a world of sounds going on around you that you simply cannot pick up with the human ear alone.

The sounds that tend to be captured, or heard, when on an investigation can be further broken down into different sub-categories, such as knocks, voices, footsteps, bangs, and so on. Some of these audible experiences can be picked up using other pieces of equipment, such as a video camera. This may not have the listening range of an advanced EVP recorder, but it may certainly help to confirm something that you thought you may have heard when listening back to your recordings after the investigation.

Knocks can be heard randomly, of course, but I find that these are harder to prove when it comes to confirming them to be a paranormal occurrence. For me, the best type of knock, tap or bang that you can experience is when it is in response to your activities. For example, you may wish to knock three times and ask if the spirits can return that particularly pattern. Another example is asking for a yes and no response by way of knocking; two knocks for yes, one knock for no. Should a knock be heard at this point, then it certainly becomes interesting when it comes to it being potentially paranormal and is worthy of more investigation.

One thing to be careful of here, though, is the natural noise of your surroundings. Before any investigation gets underway, it is always a good idea to have a walk around the area in an effort to acclimatise yourself with the noises that you may find yourself encountering throughout the night. There could be an old boiler that makes a banging noise at intermittent points throughout the investigation or there could be a leaky tap giving the impression of paranormal activity. Doing this can help when it comes to being in the thick of an investigation and trying to debunk certain noises or sounds.

One of the most recent experiences that I have encountered regarding what I call "intelligent knocking" was during an investigation at Guys Cliffe House in Warwick. This was a fascinating location, steeped in history and now predominantly used as a Freemason Lodge.

Towards the end of what had been a rather quiet investigation, a group of us were in the old cellar part of the location. Access down the steps is via an old, studded, wooden door. We were stood outside of the door with the steps on the other side and decided to knock on the door to see if we could get a response. After several attempts, and as we were about to leave the area, we heard a faint knock coming from inside the room. The sound was so faint that we had barely heard it. We decided to knock again and after several seconds the sound was returned. At this point we decided that one of the group members should go and stand at the bottom of the steps on the other side of the door to see if they could hear the knocking more clearly. It was also to see if they could recognise an echo that may have helped to explain what we were hearing. One of the members volunteered and took their place, awaiting our knocks. Once they were ready, we knocked the door and awaited a response. Once again, after several seconds, we heard the knocks being returned. When we shouted out to ask the person inside the room what they had heard, they confirmed that they could hear the return knocks but that they were finding it difficult to pinpoint where exactly the sound had been coming from.

After several more call and responses, we swapped the volunteer in the hope that they could help locate the source of the knocking. We were able to rule out echoing because the return knocks were different in number and varied in their response time. Yet again, the second volunteer really struggled to pinpoint the exact location within the room that the knocks seemed to be coming from. They were most certainly not emanating from the door itself, which is where we were knocking. The walls within the cellar were stone and it was difficult to replicate the sound that we were hearing when knocking on the stone surface, so we were also able to rule that option out. Eventually, the knocks ceased, and we moved on with the investigation. Upon listening back to our recordings, we weren't able to capture any of the knocks, except for the knocks being made by us. This was disappointing but it was still a very interesting experience, particularly as the knocks were so mysterious in their origin yet audible to the group and responsive in their nature.

When it comes to hearing sounds like footsteps, it can be a fascinating situation to find yourself in. To potentially be hearing the steps of a once living person is definitely a strange experience. However, it is an experience that should be looked at with just as much scrutiny as any other. Sometimes, understandably, it is easy to become excited and get carried away when hearing what sounds like footsteps, or any other noise seemingly coming from a spirit, but the evidence needs to be looked at in-depth before potentially being able to claim it as something within the realms of the paranormal. One thing that must be considered is the possibility that the footsteps belong to a member of the group or potentially someone else who happens to be in and around the vicinity that you are investigating. Maybe they are unaware of what you are doing, leading to them contaminating your evidence with their footsteps and noise in general, as they innocently go about their business.

Another way to approach hearing footsteps is to think about the area that you are in at the time and the material of the floor. For example, if you are in a carpeted area and you hear what sound like footsteps being made on a harder type of floor, then it may be something else that you are hearing, and not footsteps. However, I am a believer in that the spirit world does not have similar surroundings to what we can see, which may mean that the footsteps could be made to sound different, despite being on a soft floor. This could be because in their frequency, or reality, the flooring is different, allowing their footsteps to be heard in a different way. Also, if you are in an area that is prone to echo, then it can sometimes be a member of your group who, despite being a safe distance away to not interfere with your part of the investigation, may still play a part through the echo of their actions.

Throughout this book I will give examples of experiences relating to one particular house that I was invited to investigate. Without going into too much detail of the goings on at this house, the family were extremely worried, frightened, and concerned at what they were experiencing on a daily basis. The reason I will withhold the details of the haunting is because it may be that the experiences and history there could one day form another book, and I wouldn't want to repeat myself.

One of the absolute stand out experiences from our first visit to this house, and one that the group still talks of regularly to this day, was the three distinct footsteps that everyone present at the time heard coming from the landing. At the time that we heard these footsteps everyone in the house was gathered downstairs in the living room area participating in a spirit board session. There was no one else in the house apart from the people that were participating in the spirit board experiment. Throughout the evening we had regularly heard what sounded like scratching coming from the floor upstairs. The scratching noise sounded similar to what a mouse might make when burrowing, and I did enquire as to whether they had ever had a rodent problem before. The family confirmed that they had not, and there didn't seem to be any further evidence to suggest that this might be an issue. The noises always seemed to be coming from the same area, which was the main bedroom. As the living room is below the bedroom, it was also clearly audible when in the living room. However, the noise that we heard in this instance was most definitely not the scratching sound that we had been hearing. Whilst conducting the spirit board session we heard three footsteps from upstairs on the landing, followed closely by a bedroom door creaking open. I immediately ran up the stairs as fast as possible, quickly followed by everyone else, to find that no one else was up there, confirming what we had already known.

The reason we were confident in saying that they were footsteps was because of the creaking of the floorboards that we could hear when we were downstairs. As mentioned previously, it is always important to make sure that you are aware of your surroundings and the potential noises that you may hear throughout an investigation. We had already made a note that the stairs and landing were extremely creaky, just in case we decided to split the group up at some point during the night. Following the experience, we spent some time trying to reconstruct what may have caused the sound and the only thing that came anywhere near replicating what we had heard was when a member of the group walked across the landing and entered the bedroom. The group went downstairs whilst I remained on the landing walking backwards and forwards and opening the bedroom door. The group confirmed that the noise I was making was the exact same noise that we had heard previously. Interestingly, we had set up a camera at the top of the stairs and, although we didn't capture the sound of the steps, for whatever reason, we did capture the door opening, which further helped cement in our minds that we had indeed experienced footsteps walking across the landing and entering the bedroom.

If hearing footsteps can be counted as a fascinating experience to have, then surely hearing the sound of a disembodied voice is even better. Those that have encountered this experience will no doubt agree with me that this is certainly one of the best experiences that can be had when it comes to the paranormal. This can be made even better if it is able to be caught on an audible recording device for evidence and further analysis.

As with all experiences, they have to be analysed, scrutinised, and really examined before the conclusion of it being paranormal can be potentially accepted. Voices tend to differ to most other audible experiences when it comes to trying to debunk them. A knock or even footsteps are very easy to explain away, and to a hard-nosed sceptic they will quite often be dismissed as being nothing to do with the paranormal. However, a voice is a little more difficult to explain or dismiss so easily, particularly if there are words used as opposed to the sound being that of a cough, a whistle, or a humming type of sound.

One thing to consider when encountering a disembodied voice is that of your fellow group members. Always do your best to try and rule out that it was not one of them that could have made the sound, even involuntarily. Also, ensure that there are no televisions within the vicinity or phones and walkie-talkies that could be giving the impression of a ghostly voice. It is also important to remember that the human mind will try to detect patterns or try to make something out of a random sound. This falls into the phenomenon known as pareidolia, a phenomenon that I have already covered in detail in my previous book and will come back to throughout this book. Pareidolia plays a huge part in the psychology of paranormal investigating and should always be at the forefront of considerations when analysing evidence, as should any psychological behaviour. A random sound could indeed come across like a voice that is speaking words, but it could just be the mind trying to make sense of what it is hearing. This is why capturing the sound on a recorder could prove to be vital, as having the ability to listen to the piece of evidence several times could help clarify whether what someone heard was indeed paranormal or not. It is also important to try and listen to the captured evidence before allowing anyone to tell you what they can hear from the recording. This happens all too often, where an individual's perception of what they are listening to has already been shaped and predetermined by someone else, causing them to struggle to hear anything other than what they have been told to hear. I always find it fascinating when people listen to the same recording individually, without any prior clue as to what they may hear. Comparing their reactions and thoughts is always interesting. If several people claim to hear the same thing, then it can help confirm what is actually being said, but if each response is different, then it can leave the evidence confusing.

Whilst I have experienced many audible encounters throughout my time as a paranormal investigator, they are always better when they are on a personal level. The most recent personal audible experience came whilst I was actually giving a presentation to a group. The presentation was based around my previous book and was being given to a group in a café in Bristol. The chairman of the group asked if he could record the presentation, to which I gladly agreed. At one point, whilst talking to the group, I distinctly heard someone call my name. I paused what I was saying, expecting someone in the audience to have a question for me. When no one responded, I carried on with the presentation and thought nothing else of it.

A few weeks after the event, the chairman sent me the recording and pointed out a particular moment, asking me what my thoughts were. When I listened to the clip that he was referring to I was utterly amazed to actually hear someone say my name, to which I then responded to at the time of the recording. This was a fantastic piece of evidence that had managed to capture what I thought I had heard at that moment in time. When I asked him if he could remember anyone calling my name whilst I was speaking, he said that it didn't stick out to him that someone had, and the recording had come as just as much of a surprise to him when listening back to it than me when I had heard it.

Of course, it could very well have been a member of the audience calling my name, but if that were the case then why did they not respond when I paused my talking to allow them to ask their question? Also, why had the chairman not heard it at the time of the recording? To have evidence that backs up what you were convinced happened is always a satisfying feeling.

Although a whistle may not be a spoken word, it can still be counted as a disembodied voice, particularly when the whistle is in response to your own. This very scenario occurred whilst in the basement of the local pub that we have been investigating for a while now and building a case study around. The cellar is a very active part of the location, although it is also a very noisy area due to the fans and machinery that are required to keep the drinks that are stored down there cool. Whilst down there we decided to try a call and response session to see if we could interact with the spirits. After several attempts of calling out and receiving no reply, I asked if the spirits would return my whistle. Around ten seconds after I whistled, a short, melodic whistle was heard. At the time there were five of us in the cellar and every single one of us called out asking if we had all heard the whistle, which we had done. The whistle was heard over the noise of the fans in the cellar, which is a difficult thing to achieve in itself. All of the people that were present at the time claimed that they had heard the whistle and that it had sounded as if the noise had been made right next to them, despite the five of us being separated significantly enough for it to be impossible for the whistle to have emanated right next to each one of us. We have since investigated the cellar on numerous occasions but have yet to experience any noise that is as clear as the whistle was on that night.

Another report of voices being heard comes from the family home in Essex. The entity there is not a very nice one and seems to have a habit of mimicking the family voices. Now, this is a fascinating report and one that is often aligned with hauntings of a dark entity.

In this particular instance, the family have reported hearing the voice of a family member despite the fact that they are not present in the house at that time. There have been moments where Lee has been out of the house, yet Kelly has heard him calling from upstairs, using words that Lee would never use, but would be used by the children. I believe this to be the spirit's way of trying too hard to "fit in" yet getting it completely wrong. They have also reported the sound of children's laughter despite the young children not being in the house at the time.

Even the dog is mimicked, with claims of the dog barking even when the dog is out for a walk or in the same room as the family and clearly not responsible for the barking that they are hearing. I did ask if there could possibly be a neighbour's dog that they could be hearing but there isn't, and they claimed to know that the barking was that of their own dog. I know this may sound strange, but I do understand how they can recognise the bark of their own dog.

This isn't a very nice situation to be in. Having a spirit that is trying to trick the family into thinking they are hearing the voice of a fellow family member, despite them not being in the house at the time, shows the intelligence of this entity. It also highlights, in my opinion, the malicious nature of this entity, of which more will become clear as the book progresses.

Category Two: Sensory Experiences

Paranormal experiences are a very personal experience and can appear differently to each and every person, despite them potentially sharing the same experience. They can also have a different impact on each individual, making one person have completely contrasting emotions and thoughts to the next person. In my opinion, besides being attacked by a spirit, a sensory experience is about as personal an experience that you can have. By sensory, what I mean is feeling a friendly touch, sensing that something is stood next to you or in your personal space, smelling something that you should not be able to smell or feeling a hot or cold spot that should not be there. These are just a few examples of what a sensory experience could be.

As detailed in my previous book, my theory of how spirits are operating on frequencies that lie outside of our perceptive range, also known as visible light, goes a long way in helping to understand how sensory experiences can occur, despite not being able to see whatever it is that you are interacting with, or whatever is interacting with you. There will have been times, I do not doubt, where you will have experienced the sensation that you are not alone, even if you have never been on a paranormal investigation. You may have been at home, seemingly alone, but felt that someone was in the same room as you. Maybe you had the feeling that someone had entered the room, but that someone never materialises. It is examples such as this that show the restrictiveness of our perception and the five-sense reality that we are existing within. When you begin to understand that we can only interact with, and see, such a tiny amount of the world around us, then a whole plethora of possibilities opens up to you as an investigator and a researcher of the paranormal.

The problem that we face, and this stretches to the majority of humans, not just paranormal investigators, is that we seem to accept that what we can see, touch, and hear is all that there is. It is these self-imposed limitations that prevent us from truly experiencing the outer limits where these entities, energies, spirits or whatever you choose to call them exist. To give an example to what I am saying, try and remember a time where you may have felt that there was something stood next to you or near to you. That feeling may have been extremely intense, to the point where you were absolutely adamant that there was something next to you. However, when you look, using your human eyes, and therefore your limited perception, you may not see a thing. Does this mean, therefore, that there is nothing there at all? To most people, unfortunately, yes it does. What will happen in this instance is that some people will convince themselves that there is nothing near to them, simply because they cannot see it, despite what they are sensing. Now, take the points that I have mentioned above regarding the vast amount of the world that we cannot perceive, and apply them to this same situation. All of a sudden, there is a very real chance that there is, in fact, something stood near to them, but it is operating on frequency levels outside of their extremely limited range of perception.

Of course, it is not always a paranormal reason as to why you may have a sense that there is something near to you. There are plenty of other reasons that could be leading to this kind of feeling. One of the biggest is that of a psychological reaction. There are times that people can convince themselves so much that there is something near them that they become almost paranoid with it and allow their subconscious feelings to dictate their perception, giving them false experiences. This is seen often with children who may be afraid of the dark, particularly when trying to sleep, and convince themselves that there are monsters in their bedroom. Even I have, as an adult, convinced myself that the chair in the corner of the bedroom looks exactly like the shadow of a person. Despite knowing full well that it is only a chair, it can still be an unsettling feeling.

Being touched by an unseen force is, without doubt, one of the strangest sensations and experiences there is to be had when investigating the paranormal. It is something that the human brain can really struggle with when it comes to trying to explain what it possibly could be, particularly when there is nothing apparently there to touch you in the first place.

Again, as with all sensory experiences, the sensation of being touched is an extremely personal experience. Sometimes people who are investigating together can all share a particular experience, such as seeing a shadow or hearing a noise. Even the sensation of something being in the same room can be shared by people. However, it is very rare that multiple people will be touched at the same time. Of course, throughout an investigation there will be claims of such a sensation by most guests, no doubt, but it will be at different times throughout the investigation. Being touched by any living person can, to some people, be very personal. Some people value their personal space and, for whatever reason that is valid to them, are quite strict when it comes to being touched. I completely understand this point of view. There was a guest on a previous investigation who had been having the feeling of being touched and watched throughout the entire night. When we spoke about their experiences at the end of the event, they claimed that they had felt almost violated by the experience, even though the touches weren't violent in any way. This is what I mean by it being a very personal experience for some people. What makes it worse is that you are, in most cases, being touched by something that you cannot see, which is considerably different to being touched by someone that you can see because at least in that instance you can move away from that person and the situation.

There are ways to help in this kind of situation, which, of course, we informed this particular individual of at the time. One way to help yourself cope is to tell the spirits that you do not wish to be touched or interacted with in that way in the hope that they respect what you have said and leave you be. Sometimes this can work, but there are times that the spirits persist in their actions, which can become extremely frustrating for the individual that is being affected. Another thing you could try is to work on your protection. I know that the whole protection scenario isn't a great fit for everyone, and that there are people who do not fully believe in what it claims to do, but for those that do participate in it, then using it to push away unwanted attention is another possible solution to the problem.

When it comes to protection, its purpose, and its validity, on a personal level, I am not a complete believer in its effectiveness. I understand that this may not sit right with some people who are reading this and that is absolutely fine. I respect all opinions and thoughts on anything associated with the paranormal field. You should by now be fully aware of my theories and research into the nature of reality and how we perceive the world around us, and how this fits into the paranormal world and my research in that respect. Part of this is having an understanding of how we are creating our own reality and how we manifest our own beliefs into our daily lives. For example, isn't it strange how often a religious person will be visited by, or be witness to, a manifestation of a religious figure, such as the Virgin Mary? Very rarely is she witnessed by someone who has no connection to her or no religious beliefs whatsoever.

Protecting yourself can sometimes involve a form of meditation. This can be done as an individual or as part of a group, where you may, to give an example, imagine a white light washing over your entire body and surrounding you in order to prevent the spirits from coming too close to you or being able to interact with you in a way that you would not like. There are also other ways to practice protection, but this is just one example. Some people believe that paranormal experiences are all psychological and are only taking place in the experiencer's mind. This may be correct, but I would go as far to say that what is actually happening is that the paranormal experience, which is most certainly happening for the experiencer, is now existing within the experiencer's perception of reality, which they create and therefore have created the paranormal experience itself. My point is that with protection being inside the individual's mind, also, then it stands to reason that the person will simply trick themselves into thinking that they are safe and therefore will be safe. If they do not believe themselves to be safe from spiritual contact, then they will create a situation in which something will happen to them to further their belief that they are not protected, such as being touched by a spirit.

This leads me on to how even the feeling of being touched cannot always be considered paranormal without considering other options first. Sometimes, as I have witnessed first-hand, people on investigations can get themselves into such a state of fear or paranoia that they begin to believe that they are being touched, watched, or followed, when it is all in their own mind. Of course, who am I to say that what they tell me they are experiencing isn't true? This I understand, but if someone is convinced that they are going to be touched, I truly believe that there will be times where they have created that experience themselves. It could also be something as simple as clothing. I remember an investigation where I was convinced that my back was constantly being touched and that my shirt was being tugged at throughout the majority of the investigation. This didn't end up being the case, though, as I eventually realised that my hoody was partly tucked inside my jeans, which is what was causing the tugging sensation whenever I leaned forward or twisted my body. As soon as I pulled my hoody out of my jeans the seemingly paranormal activity ceased.

One sensory experience, where the feeling of being touched was a common theme throughout the entire group, occurred in Drakelow Tunnels. The network of tunnels at this location is vast, stretching for miles. One of the areas within the tunnels is a small room that is known as the Key Room, supposedly where a security officer used to be based. We have conducted several experiments in this particular room, mainly calling out. It was during one of these sessions, whilst we were all stood in a circle, that people began to experience the feeling that something was brushing against their legs. Several people claimed to have experienced this during this one session. Furthermore, the group that followed us, having had no prior communication with us about what we had experienced whilst in the room before them, also made the same claims that there was something brushing against their legs. To make matters more interesting, we have had these claims from different groups across different investigations. When this happens, it becomes very interesting because the experience is repeating with different people. The chances of different people, in different groups, on different events experiencing the same sensory activity is extremely slim, so is certainly worth investigating from a paranormal angle.

Someone pointed out that a security guard would have more than likely had a dog with him whilst on duty. This is a very good point, and likely to be true. Could it be, then, that the thing brushing against people's legs when in the room could actually be the spirit of a dog that once kept the security guard company. I have considered that it may have been a live animal that was dwelling in the tunnels at the time. The problem with this theory is that I have not once seen a live animal in the tunnels, despite investigating there plenty of times. Also, people were shining torches during the experience to see if they could show what was causing the feeling, yet they could see nothing. This leads me to believe that the experiences, having been shared across multiple groups on different occasions, is that of a paranormal experience.

Experiencing a smell that you feel you should not be smelling, or appears unnatural at the time, can indeed be a strange experience but can actually be rather commonplace within the paranormal investigative field. When people think about the sensory experiences that they might encounter when interacting with the paranormal, they quite often forget that smelling is not only one of them but can play an integral part. Everybody considers feeling something, hearing something, and seeing something but it is very rare that they consider the sense of smell and the part that it can play. Imagine being in a room that used to be used for a particular purpose and picking up on that smell when investigating it. Another possibility is having known someone before they died, someone who may have had a distinctive smell due to the particular perfume or deodorant that they wore and being able to smell them every now and again.

It is important to note, though, that there are health and psychological conditions that can cause an individual to smell something that is not actually there. This is known as phantom smells or phantosmia. This can be harmless the majority of the time, causing the person being affected to smell something such as burnt toast or a metallic smell, but it can also be a sign of a much deeper health concern. Sinusitis, migraines, strokes and even brain tumours have all been linked to this strange condition. Psychologically, it is important to know that the sense of smell is very closely linked to memory. Simply remembering a scene from your past can invoke a particular smell that is clearly not there at the time of remembering but is all in the mind. Of course, it can also happen the other way around, in that an actual smell could trigger a particular memory. I don't want to get too bogged down in the science here, but some really quick research will show you how the sense of smell is linked to the limbic system, which is a set of structures within the brain that are regarded as being a huge part of memory storing.

It may seem like I am going a little too deep here, but it really is important to consider any psychological aspects when it comes to trying to prove or disprove the existence of the paranormal.

My parents believe that their house is regularly visited by my dad's aunty, Beryl. There are several reasons that have led them to believe that she visits them, one being a distinctive smell that is often lingering in the downstairs area. I only met Beryl a handful of times as a very young child before she died, so I don't personally remember too much about her. One thing I do remember, though, was her distinct smell. As a school dinner lady who used to pride herself on her appearance, she would often have a strange smell that seemed to be a combination of grease, from spending all day cooking school dinners, and perfume. It was a very odd smell indeed and unique to her. There are times at my parents' house that you can walk downstairs and be hit with this incredibly unmistakable smell. Interestingly, it always seems to linger in the same area, and never travels upstairs. Also, it always seems to occur in the morning and never any other time of the day.

Is this actually proof that Beryl is haunting the house and visiting my parents? Quite possibly it is, but it could also be a memory that is triggered and causes the smell to occur, as mentioned previously. For example, in their living room there are several ornaments that my parents inherited from Beryl following her death. Could it be that seeing these ornaments upon entering the living room triggers a memory, without even knowing it, and so the smell quickly follows? I would argue that this could definitely be a cause, but there have also been moments of activity with these ornaments that have caught our attention. There have been several occasions where the candle holders have been seen, and heard, shuffling across the coffee table in the living room. There has never been an explanation that I can come up with to explain how these items were able to move in the way that they did. I even went as far as placing a spirit level on the coffee table to see if there was a potential slope that may cause the ornaments to move, but it was perfectly level. Placing this activity with the smell that has accompanied the arrival of these ornaments certainly leads me to believe that there is more to it than just the memory triggering the smell.

Temperature changes can be a big indication of paranormal activity, supposedly. Feeling a hot or cold spot is, according to some people, a clear sign that there is a spirit or entity nearby. Plenty of people have been on investigations and claimed that they can feel a cold area that is otherwise surrounded by warmer air. There are also regular claims that their hand, or another part of their body, has dropped or increased in temperature.

There are, of course, plenty of reasons for this kind of sensation happening that have nothing to do with the paranormal whatsoever. It is always important when first scoping a location to ensure that there are no draughts around. If there are, and this cannot be helped in some locations that are older or more run-down, then making a note of it and the area that the draught is in will ensure that there are no inaccurate claims throughout the investigation. Also, the feeling of being anxious or on edge when investigating, which can happen frequently, can be a cause of temperature changes within the human body. Anxiety can cause changes to the heart rate which can affect the blood being pumped around the body and therefore affect an individual's temperature. Again, this is another example of how psychology can impact results when investigating the paranormal and how experiences need to be researched deeper instead of being taken at face value.

Throughout my research I must admit that I have struggled to come across any solid evidence to suggest that a sudden drop or rise in the ambient temperature of a location is in any way related to paranormal activity.

During one of the investigations at my local pub, a location that I have spoken of at length in my previous book, there was a particular moment where the group could feel a cold area in the bar section. The area in question isn't usually a part of the pub that we spend any time in during an investigation, but we do pass through there on the way to other areas. It was whilst we were walking through the bar area that a few people mentioned that they could feel a cold spot. Upon investigating further, it became clear that there was definitely a colder area that seemed to have a radius of around a meter. We used our temperature gun on the area, and it showed that it was around four degrees colder than any other part of the bar. The use of the temperature gun is very important, because there can be a huge psychological aspect at play during situations such as this, where susceptible people can be led to feel, hear, or see something that isn't actually there, because other members of the group have said that there is. If you have been on regular investigations, then you will understand what I am saying. There are certainly times where one person's opinion can lead to everyone else having the same opinion.

Later in the investigation we were down in the cellar of the pub participating in some calling out, hoping to get a response, when someone mentioned how cold the cellar had become. Of course, the cellar is always cold due to the cooling equipment that is required in order to keep the drinks cold. At this point, another member of the team asked if it was possible that the area in the bar, where we had previously felt the cold spot, was above the cooler in the cellar. A couple of us headed upstairs into the bar area and towards where the cold spot was still lingering. Once in position we stamped our feet several times to alert the rest of the group below in the cellar that we were in the right place. We then headed back into the cellar and asked the group to point out where they had heard our stamping coming from. They all pointed towards the air conditioning unit. In that moment we knew that we had solved the mystery of the cold spot in the bar area. The air conditioning was causing cold air to travel through the ceiling of the cellar, into the bar area and causing a cold area to develop.

Category Three: Visual Experiences

Visual experiences can come in many forms and, as is the case with most of these categories, they can cross over into another form of experience. For example, seeing an item move or be thrown by an invisible force is a visual experience, but in addition to that, can be classed as interference, also. However, managing to capture something moving, being thrown, or being interacted with is a very rare occurrence when on investigations. Most visual experiences can be classed as seeing orbs or shadows, with a very occasional part or full-body manifestation.

When it comes to visual experiences, one of the most commonly reported is that of orbs. These tiny manifestations are rarely visible when it comes to seeing them with the naked eye and are mostly spotted on photographs or video footage taken. They can vary in shape, size and brightness but are always noticeable on videos by their fluid, independent movements that make them stand out from the possibility of them being just another dust particle. Confusing paranormal orbs with dust is a very common mistake that is made, yet it is very easy to do so. One thing I always try and consider is whether the orb in question is displaying any independent movements and has the ability to change direction. On most videos, dust will be easily visible as it reflects the light from the camera. The dust particles will also tend to all be flowing in the same general direction, being blown by a faint breeze or draught. However, when an orb begins to act differently and of its own accord, moving in a different direction, then it deserves more attention and a closer look. Sometimes it may catch your eye simply because it is bigger or brighter than the dust particles, as well as moving freely and independently. It is when this happens that I believe there is a possible chance of the orb being paranormal. The reason I only say possible here is because we can truly never know if it is a paranormal orb or not.

With that being said, there is always another possibility and that is that you are capturing an insect on film. This would certainly help to explain the independent movement and the going against the dust particles that you may be seeing. Always bear this in mind when pondering whether an orb you have captured on film is truly paranormal or not.

When it comes to capturing orbs on photographs, the most common mistake is assuming that a reflection of light on to the camera lens is a paranormal orb. This is known as a lens flare and is quite common on photographs in general. It is easy to see why these discrepancies may be mistaken for paranormal orbs but must always be considered when analysing the evidence.

As with most pieces of evidence, I find that orbs are always more trustworthy if they appear as a reactionary response to your investigation. In this case, an orb that reacts to something you have asked or done whilst investigating is always of more interest from a paranormal perspective. It may be that you have asked a spirit to try and show themselves and an orb appears on your film or photograph. If this does happen, then it certainly makes you think twice about what it is that you may be seeing.

Our recent investigation of the family home in Essex gave us several great examples of reactionary responses when it comes to the manifestation and the interaction of orbs. We had a camera set up on the top of the stairs, which was focused on a trigger object that we had set up, in the hope of capturing some movement throughout the night. Although it never did manage to capture the trigger object moving, this particular camera gave us some really good pieces of evidence. This was the camera that I mentioned earlier that had managed to capture the door opening after the footsteps had occurred on the landing.

When it came to capturing orbs, it did a very good job for us. One piece of video footage shows two bright points of light shoot across the hallway and head down the stairs at an alarming speed. At the time that this had happened we were all downstairs laughing. You can hear the laughter in the background on the video footage. A lot of people claim that laughter helps when on an investigation, but in this instance, where the energy is quite dark, I believe it can also serve to irritate the entity, but that certainly does not mean that laughter is not welcome. Absolutely not. What this video seemed to show was two orbs reacting to our laughter and then heading down the stairs to see what was going on. At the time of the orbs appearing on the video footage there is no other visual evidence occurring, such as dust particles, which is what makes this particular instance of so much interest.

Another piece of evidence that we were fortunate enough to get from this camera involved another two orbs shooting through the legs of one of our group members as they opened up one of the bedroom doors. From watching the video clip, it seems as if the orbs were waiting for the door to be opened before they could enter the bedroom. As one of our group members opens the door, two bright orbs appear from nowhere and travel between his legs, entering the bedroom. Are these the same two orbs that were captured heading down the stairs towards our laughter? It is almost impossible to say, but it is interesting that there were two again.

Further cementing the possibility that it was the same two orbs that the camera kept on capturing is the fact that there was a third piece of evidence caught on the same camera, again involving two orbs. This time the two orbs seem to be reacting to something I had asked. On the video footage you can hear me call out and ask if the spirit could copy my knocking, at which point I knock on the landing banister. Several seconds after I have made the knocking noise, two orbs appear from nowhere and start floating around the hand that I had knocked with. At first I did wonder if the knocking could have caused some dust to begin floating around, but the two orbs are too bright, as well as displaying independent movement

What I find particularly interesting with these examples is that there is clearly no evidence of dust contamination on any of the footage both before and after the orbs show themselves. The lights also seem to be acting completely independently and reactionary, which certainly makes them worthy of attention. Is it possible that the orbs were simply two insects that were hanging around on the landing and reacting to sounds such as the laughter and knocking? It is very possible, but after studying the videos numerous times, I cannot seem to make out any wings which are sometimes visible if the supposed orb is in fact an insect, which leaves me to conclude that it may actually be, in this case, paranormal.

One of the most fascinating orb experiences that we were lucky enough to capture on video footage happened in Drakelow Tunnels. The kitchen area is one of my favourite parts of the location, as we always seem to get some kind of activity there, ranging from spirit board interaction to physical contact.

During this particular session in the kitchen area, we decided to play some 1940's music in the hope that it would bring about some interaction with the spirits, should they hear music from their era. To further try and bring about some interaction, we decided to begin dancing to the music to see what response we could get. The video footage shows me and another member of the group dancing to the music whilst dust is clearly visible moving from the ground upwards, having been disrupted by our dancing. A short while into the video, a red orb makes an appearance and moves around me at waist height, towards the camera and moves off to the right of the screen. As the orb gets closer to the camera, it becomes obvious that there are, in fact, two small orbs moving around each other, almost as if they are dancing. The orb was witnessed live by the group members holding the camera, and their amazement is clear to hear in their voices as they spot the dancing lights.

The fact that the orbs are red in colour makes them stand out against the wave of dust that is being created by our dancing. Also, the orbs begin their journey at waist height, so they have clearly not been kicked up from the ground as the dust has been. The way they moved around me is as if they are showing intelligent movement, avoiding bumping into me as they may have done had they been a living person. Finally, the fact that there are actually two orbs seemingly intertwining with each other as if dancing, really makes this an incredible piece of footage.

Photographs have the ability to often throw up some interesting shapes and colours that can be often mistaken for being paranormal. Mist or smoke seems to be a common occurrence when it comes to people presenting photographs as evidence that they have indeed captured something from the spirit world.

One thing that needs to be considered when it comes to studying evidence containing a mist like image is the environment in which the photograph was taken. For example, if it is taken outside then what could have been captured could be nothing more than a natural mist or fog. It may even be the remnants of breath after breathing out on a particularly cold evening. This tends to be very similar to fog when photographed and has an opaque, wispy look to it. I have even been on outdoor investigations with people who are smoking. Whilst I do not have a particular issue with this, it does tend to add another element of possibilities when it comes to trying to understand what you have photographed and the reasoning behind why you have captured something that resembles a mist. It is also important to point out here that there is no reason to think that a mist has any relation whatsoever to paranormal activity. The same can be said for orbs, to a certain point. There is no evidence to suggest that seeing an orb or a mist correlates directly to witnessing any form of paranormal activity. If there are other pieces of activity happening around the same time, or if the visual piece of evidence can be tied into something related to your investigation, such as the reactionary responses from orbs that I mentioned earlier, then it can be looked at with a little more confidence from a paranormal perspective.

Of course, the biggest issue with capturing what looks like paranormal activity on a photograph is whether the equipment being used is potentially faulty or not. A faulty, or dirty, camera lens could quite easily throw out some misleading photographs that may cause you to believe that you have captured something not of this world, when in fact it is simply because your equipment is faulty. However, this should be easy to spot and rectify. If you begin to notice that more and more pictures have a similar apparition of sorts, always appearing in the same position in the picture, then make sure to check the camera that you are using and ensure that it is not the fault of the equipment before jumping to any paranormal conclusions.

A recent outdoor investigation of a local cemetery gave us some really good photographic evidence, one of which I will discuss later in this chapter. Another one of the photographs that we captured that night seems to show a solid, white mass covering half of the picture. We took around a dozen or so pictures in one particular area in quick succession. There was no longer than a second or two between each picture being taken, yet the discrepancy only appeared on one of the many photographs. Whenever this occurs, it is an instant attention grabber.

What was particularly interesting with this picture was just how solid this mist looked. It had a very clear shape to it and was not transparent in the slightest. The background was completely blocked out by this shape. We were lucky enough to spot this pretty much instantly, so decided to try and rule out any other possibilities. As the night was very cold, I exhaled in front of the camera and took multiple pictures to see if what we had caught could possibly have been someone's breath finding its way in front of the camera. When reviewing the pictures, we quickly realised that what we had caught could not possibly be someone's breath. The picture of my exhaled breath was extremely wispy and was almost entirely see-through, allowing the background of the picture to be seen very clearly. When comparing this to the solid shape we had caught on camera a short while before, it clearly showed to us that what we had caught was certainly not breath. Another factor that convinced us of this was that the multiple pictures that we had taken of my breath showed evidence of the wispy trail for several pictures. However, with the strange picture we were trying to replicate, the white mist appeared for only one photograph, meaning it had to manifest and then disappear again in no longer than two seconds or so.

Another possible cause for what we had caught is that it was an insect. This may help to explain how it only appeared very briefly for one shot before disappearing again in the next one and may also explain the solid appearance that the shape had. My only concern with this theory is that of all of the pictures that we had taken that night, of which there were hundreds, not one other photo shows any sign of having this type of apparition.

My conclusion on this photograph still remains cautious, as there is no leading proof either way, but it is certainly a strange manifestation given all of the processes that we followed in order to try and debunk it.

Another visual experience that is commonly encountered on investigations, as well as in everyday life, is that of seeing a shadow. Shadows are often caught out of the corner of an investigator's eye or passing across doorways. A lot of sightings also consist of a shadow lurking in the corner of a room. These shadows are very rarely confrontational and tend to keep their distance, lurking just out of reach, as if keeping an eye on you or checking out what you are up to.

There are some interesting pieces of equipment that can help capture shadows, including the obvious video recorder or camera, where pictures have often caught these shadowy figures presenting themselves. Another piece of equipment is a laser grid pen. This enables shadows to be spotted much more easily, particularly when in extremely dark locations, where shadows may otherwise be difficult to spot. It also works well as a backdrop for photographs and video footage, as it allows darker shapes to be spotted more easily on the bright background.

Shadows are such a prominent feature in evidence that is collected from paranormal investigations that they even have their own phenomenon where they are known most commonly as Shadow People. There are several researchers in the field that specialise in the research of these Shadow People and I urge you to take a further look into the phenomenon, as it is very interesting indeed. When researching, you may come across the most famous of all Shadow People – the Hat Man. This particular shadowy figure seems to haunt many people around the world, often accompanying a form of sleep paralysis or nightmare around the time that he appears.

Whilst Shadow People seem to be independent paranormal entities, most people believe that shadows in general are a basic form of manifestation when it comes to spirits trying to show themselves. I do always wonder, though, if a spirit is trying to show themselves, why are shadows mostly so cautious when it comes to making themselves known? Hiding away in the corner or tucked behind a door frame doesn't help if their intention is to interact with those that are investigating them.

When on paranormal investigations, the lights will usually be off, leading to some very dark areas. This naturally leads people to use torches, primarily as a health and safety precaution. Some locations that you may find yourself investigating are centuries old and can be very dangerous when trying to navigate in total darkness. Whilst the use of torches and other lighting can aid in the safety of an investigation, it can also present false evidence when it comes to experiences such as shadows. The shadows being cast by the light of the torches can often be mistaken for a paranormal entity revealing itself. One thing to bear in mind is that if you have split up your group in order to cover multiple areas of a location at the same time, then there may be times that their lights can be seen from where your group is investigating, even if you think that you are far enough away from the other group to prevent any cross contamination. There may also be times where, although you may not be able to see their lights, you will see shadows that are being cast by their torches. There will be other light sources that need to be kept in mind, too, if you begin to experience shadows. Most locations will have emergency lighting, fire exit and general exit signs around the areas that you will be investigating. A lot of these locations prohibit you from altering these lights and covering them up as it could invalidate insurance and prevent them from doing the job they are intended to do, which is of course to guide you to safety in an emergency.

On top of these light sources potentially giving false evidence, there is also the outside to consider. If a location is near to a busy road, then the cars that will be passing by need to be considered, as well as the streetlights that may be directly outside the windows. If the windows are not completely covered, then these are other light sources that could contaminate any evidence gathered from an investigation. Many locations that I have investigated have been at the mercy of outside contamination and it can lead to a rather frustrating investigation, as nothing can truly be trusted due to the fact that you are always having to consider the possibility that it was a light or a noise from outside.

Over the course of many investigations, I have been a witness to many shadows appearing not only on photographs and video recordings, but also in front of my own eyes. There have been times where I am the only one in a room full of people who seems to be able to see a shadow maneuvering around us. On the other hand, there have been many times where it has been the complete other way around and no matter what people tell me they are witnessing I just cannot see what they are seeing. As I have said time and time again, this does not mean that they are right, and I am wrong. The longer I spend investigating the paranormal the more I become convinced that each and every experience is a personal experience to the individual. There may be times that a particular experience can be shared, and that is a great feeling, as it helps to confirm what you are seeing, but on the whole, an experience is personal, and should be treated as such. As mentioned in my previous book, I believe this to be down to the way each individual perceives their own reality and the frequencies that they are able to tune in to in order to receive these experiences.

One of the first pieces of video footage I was sent from the family who's house I have been investigating was that of a shadow. It remains, to this day, one of the most intriguing pieces of evidence that I have ever had the fortune to see. For those of you who have seen my presentation live or watched one of my online presentations, you will know the video I am alluding to, but for those that have not, I will do my very best to describe the footage here.

The video begins with Lee, the man of the house who seems to really upset the entity that is there, filming from one end of the landing to the other. At the end of the landing there is a bedroom door on the left and the bathroom door is on the right. Lee began the filming originally because he believed that he had heard someone moving around in the bedroom. This was shortly after they had begun experiencing strange occurrences in their home, maybe a day or two after the first occurrence. During the thirty second clip Lee begins to ask the entity to show itself, calling out that he knows it is there with him. He then begins to move down the hallway towards the bedroom and bathroom doors. As he approaches the two doors, a small, imp like shadow appears to move very quickly from the bedroom door on the left across the hallway and into the bathroom door on the right. On the video footage the shadow doesn't appear to be any taller than a foot or so and presents itself as a solid, black mass. Lee doesn't seem to notice this at the time of it happening, but shortly after the shadow disappears into the bathroom the bathroom door slams shut. At this point, Lee panics and begins to back away rather quickly.

I have studied this video dozens of times and played with the speed, the light contrast and the colours in an effort to try and have a better understanding of what exactly it is that the video shows. No matter what I do to the video or how many times I watch it, there is no denying that a shadowy figure moves from the bedroom and into the bathroom before slamming the door shut behind itself. When we visited the house back in late 2019, one of the first things we were desperate to do was to try and recreate this video, just to see if we could prove that it wasn't paranormal. We made several attempts at debunking the footage but just could not seem to replicate what the footage had shown. One of the group members filmed the landing, mirroring what Lee had been doing during the video, whilst another member stood behind them trying their best to cast a shadow that was similar in shape and size to what was shown in the footage. This proved incredibly difficult to do and we gave up with no success. We also checked the bathroom door to see if it closed on its own, which it did not, as well as checking the area for any breeze or draughts that may have caused the door to close itself. Again, these attempts ended in failure and we eventually had to concede that we simply could not copy what the video footage had shown.

The holy grail of evidence, in my opinion, is being to see, and capture if possible, a full-bodied, or even part-bodied, manifestation. Anyone that has managed to do so will understand just how fantastic it feels, particularly if you are able to capture it on a photograph or a video as evidence to further analyse. If you don't manage to capture what you have experienced, then it can be a shame in that you will not have it to show other people or to help you in understanding what it is that you have seen. With that being said, at least you will have had an experience that many investigators never manage to have, despite dedicating their lives to the cause, in some cases.

There are two possibilities of experiencing a manifestation, or apparition as it is also known. The first possibility is seeing it with your own eyes, live so to speak, and capturing it, or not, once you have seen it. The second possibility is not knowing there is a manifestation occurring at the time that you are taking a picture or recording a video, only to then later find out that you have captured it without knowing. Both of these possibilities come with their own feelings and emotions that will no doubt be personal to you but will also be shared by many others who will have had a similar experience.

What is also interesting is the vast difference in what the manifestations appear to be doing whenever they choose to show themselves. Of course, there is a debate over whether the spirit is actually choosing to show themselves at the time of the experience. I would argue that, whilst they can tune in and out of our frequency range and our perception and show themselves that way, it is actually the other way around and it is us, the viewer, that has somehow managed to perceive a world outside of our frequency range for the briefest of moments and witness the world that they are inhabiting. When they are viewed, though, it is interesting that some will not even acknowledge the living people within their vicinity and just go about their tasks as if no one else is there. There are other apparitions that do appear to interact, and some willingly, with the people that are witnessing them. I find this difference in behaviour intriguing and often wonder if the behavioural difference is somehow a clue as to what type of manifestation is being experienced at that time. Some people claim that the apparitions that appear to continue about their business without paying anyone, or anything, any attention are ghosts and are a type of recording. An energy that has imprinted itself on to the fabric of time and is replaying over and over again. The apparitions that do interact with their surroundings are spirits and are an intelligent entity that has the ability to communicate with the living knowingly. I am not entirely sure that these definitions are accurate when it comes to describing what is what, but it is certainly interesting to study the difference in the way each manifestation conducts itself when being viewed.

As usual, however, each independent experience must be scrutinised before it can be truly counted as paranormal. There are several things to consider when studying the potential evidence of a full or part-bodied apparition. The first thing to consider would be that you haven't somehow managed to film or photograph another member of your group, unknowingly. Whilst you may think it would be obvious if it were a member of your group in the piece of evidence, there are certain situations that may make it difficult to ascertain as to whether it is them or not. For example, a reflection of your fellow group member in a window. This could slightly obscure the image or cause it to be slightly out of shape or of a different colour. This may trick you in to thinking that it is an apparition that has been caught on film. Also, the way that the lighting is reflecting off the camera lens, as discussed previously, could cast shadows, or light on to a living person which in turn could cause them to appear unrecognisable when it comes to viewing the evidence. Besides these points, there are plenty more to consider when looking through pieces of evidence that you may be thinking shows the manifestation of a spirit.

One manifestation experience I can recall occurred at the local pub that we have been lucky enough to investigate numerous times. This particular experience involved a fellow investigator of mine who had an experience involving the witnessing of a full-bodied apparition. The experience occurred in the cellar, which is a very active area of the pub. As detailed previously, we have experienced whistles and moving barrels in this area. I have even had my name called and a general feeling of uneasiness is often cited in the one part of the cellar. The cellar consists of two main areas, in which you can stand upright. These two areas are connected by an extremely narrow pathway, roughly twenty feet or so long. The pathway is arched overhead, meaning you have to crouch down when walking along it. At the end of one of the investigations, once all of the guests had left, a few of us decided to go and spend ten minutes just sitting in the cellar to see if we could experience anything. It had been rather active that night and we wanted one final piece of the action before we decided to head home. We entered the cellar, through the first main area, along the narrow pathway and settled down on some barrels in the second area. The way that we were sat allowed us to look along the pathway and view the other main area. After a couple of minutes or so, our eyes adjusted to the darkness and it became apparent that there was some activity in the other area. There is a little amount of light that penetrates the cellar door and ever so slightly illuminates the floor and barrels in the area. This kept going dark periodically, as if something were moving in front of it and blocking the light out. Eventually, the activity peaked when one member of the group claimed to be witnessing a full-bodied apparition. He claimed to see what he believed to be a woman, in a white dress with dark hair, moving from left to right across the main area that we were focusing on. The experience lasted for no longer than three seconds and ended with the figure disappearing into the wall on the right-hand side. The figure seemed to pay no attention to us as we were staring down towards the apparition. There were four of us in the group and Ryan was the only one to have had this experience, even though we were all focusing on the same area. When I asked him what had happened, he stated that moments before the apparition appeared, his head had begun to feel as though it was filled with static, leading him to almost expect something was going to happen. Although he claims it was a female that he witnessed, he cannot truly be sure, but believes that the figure looked feminine in nature. We spent a further few minutes down there, wishing something else to happen, particularly so that the rest of the group could witness something, but unfortunately this never happened, and we called it a night.

One of our recent investigations at the local cemetery provided us with a possible part manifestation that was caught on a photograph. Throughout the evening I was taking pictures on my smart phone of various areas within the cemetery. One picture, which I did not notice until the next day when studying the collection of photographs, seems to contain a very strange looking figure. The picture is of two tombstones next to each other. On the original picture I could just make out what originally looked like a sort of smudge above and slightly to the right of the one tombstone. At first, I thought nothing of it, but when I zoomed in, I could make more sense of the shape and begin to see what it could possibly be. I zoomed in a little further, saving each picture for comparison, and began to change the contrast and colours in order to see if the image could appear sharper and clearer. Eventually, after doing all that I could do without spoiling the picture, it became apparent that there definitely was some form of manifestation occurring above the tombstone. To my eyes it looks like a hooded figure, or someone with long hair. The top part of the body is just visible before it fades away.

I regularly use this picture in my presentations, so please take a look online for one of my presentations and no doubt you will come across it. When I do present this piece of evidence it is always interesting to hear the feedback from people on what they think it is in the picture. Some people don't think that there is anything worth noting at all, and that is absolutely fine. Others claim to see something but cannot be sure of what exactly it is they are looking at. Some people agree with my opinion, despite me never telling them what to see, as I do not believe in planting the thoughts into their minds. Whatever it may be, it was certainly a very interesting photograph to capture and one that will no doubt require further studying in the future.

Category Four: Interference Experiences

As mentioned previously, there will be certain times and certain experiences where these categories seem to cross over, and they become one and the same. Seeing something move can fall into both the visual and interference category. What I have tried to do, however, is break them up as clearly as possible, but do bear in mind that there will be cross overs.

Interference experiences are very closely related to both visual experiences and physical experiences, but they do differ enough to warrant its own category. For me, interference is when an item is moved, whether that be a trigger object that has been set up as part of an experiment whilst on an investigation, or just an everyday item that has moved without being part of an investigation. It could also be when a piece of investigative kit is interfered with, such as an EMF meter, REM pod, spirit board and so on. People will also claim to have had things moved around in their home, doors opening and closing, as well as other interference activities. Another example of interference would be items being thrown. However, I do tend to keep that particular example within the physical category due to the nature of the interference, meaning an item being thrown at you is, in my opinion, a little more extreme than just mere interference. For me, interference is simply when an entity enters into our reality and begins to interfere with items around us, as opposed to interfering directly with us, which is more of the physical aspect.

I will try not to cover the equipment being interfered with aspect of this category in too much detail, as that is essentially what my previous book was all about. However, it is important to discuss how spirits will interfere with the equipment that you are using in many different ways. Of course, interference with your equipment is pretty much the whole purpose of going out and investigating in the first place. Investigators will crave the movement of a glass on a spirit board or to see the flashing of lights on their EMF meter. Activity like this is what makes it all worthwhile. Seeing a spirit with your own eyes or hearing sounds is fantastic, but without the equipment being used there is no way of gathering the experiences as solid evidence in order to help try and prove what it was that you experienced to others. With that being said, experiences are personal by nature, and you should never feel the need to have to prove to someone what exactly it was that you experienced. By now, particularly if you have read my previous book, you will have an understanding of what equipment tends to be used when out investigating the paranormal and how that equipment works when supposedly interacting with the spirit world.

EMF meters, which measure the electromagnetic field and any disturbances to that field, will light up and flash if a spirit is nearby. REM pods will beep, flash, and make loud noises if something interferes with the electromagnetic field it is creating around itself. Spirit boards allow a spirit to communicate with us by moving a designated glass or planchette around a board consisting of numbers and letters in order to spell out what it is that they mean to say. Of course, everything I have just listed is subject to scrutiny, which I have done in previous works, so I won't go into too much detail here, but it shows how equipment being used is always interfered with by some form of energy or spirit.

There are times, though, that the interference may not be attributed to spirit activity but could simply be a piece of equipment running out of battery power. For example, there are claims that items of equipment such as laser grid pens or EMF meters can be tampered with by spirits, but it is always important to check the battery level and, if required, replace the batteries. This may help improve the performance of the equipment and show that it was nothing to do with paranormal interference to begin with. With that being said, I have experienced equipment being drained of battery power despite replacing the batteries several times throughout the investigation. When this happens, it certainly makes you think that there could be paranormal activity going on as it goes against the normal behaviour of the equipment.

When we were investigating the house in Essex, we decided to set up a spirit board at the top of the stairs. This was because the landing appeared to be the most active area of the house from previous videos, research, and experiences, and as I describe more experiences from this house, you will soon realise that the landing area is the epicentre for activity. Whilst we were conducting the spirit board session, we had an EMF meter nearby to see if it could pick up any interference. In hindsight, this was a good decision, as the EMF meter turned out to be much more active than the spirit board. Although the glass did move and answer several of our questions, it seemed that the majority of the responses were coming through the EMF meter. Just to point out, all of our mobile phones were on flight mode and I made a point of moving the camera that was being used to film the spirit board session away from the meter, to prohibit any false evidence. Interestingly, the line of questioning we ended up taking with the spirit board led us to receiving an answer that the entity we were dealing with was not human and did not come from earth. I am not entirely sure we can completely trust all answers that we receive on spirit boards because, just like humans hiding behind computers, it is easy for the entity to play games and pretend it is something that it is not or that it is much more threatening than it truly is. However, with my theory of what spirits could actually be, it is entirely possible that you will, at times, encounter an energy that has never inhabited a human body within the human frequency range.

The EMF meter was extremely active during the spirit board session, lighting up to answer questions that the glass would not move for. We eventually managed to have the meter going all up to the red light for a yes answer and only to the orange light for a no answer. This enabled us to communicate with the entity without the need of the spirit board. The meter then continued to be active throughout the entire investigation. In fact, it was possibly the most active I have ever seen an EMF meter on any of my investigations. This led me to asking the family if they had experienced any electrical issues within the house prior to our visit. I was surprised when they confirmed with me that the local council had only just come out to check themselves around three weeks before the investigation. The council confirmed that everything was absolutely fine and that there were no issues to be concerned about from an electrical point of view. The reason that the family had called the council out in the first place was because of the lights in the house constantly flashing on and off or flickering really quickly. Despite the council confirming there were no issues, the problem persisted. What was of great interest to the group was how the EMF meter only seemed to be majorly affected when on the staircase or the landing. As this seems to be the epicenter for most of the activity, I was intrigued that the meter seemed to confirm this.

Our recent investigation at Guys Cliffe House in Warwick gave us some good interference experiences with our equipment. One of our group members had a small, plastic ball that would flash different coloured lights if moved. This is a great item to be used in the dark as it gives you instant notification that it has been disturbed. One thing to be cautious of, though, is with the item being round in shape, it would be very easy for it to move by itself if not placed in a steady and safe position. This could lend itself to giving the illusion of it being interfered with by a spirit, when in fact it has just rolled due to being placed insecurely on an uneven surface.

During this particular investigation, we were having a lot of responses on our EMF meter whilst in the outside stables area. This was interesting in itself because there is no electricity out there and we were far enough away from the main building for any interference to be coming from there. The EMF meter kept leading us down a path as if someone were trying to take us somewhere. If we stopped along the path or deviated into one of the side rooms, then the meter would stop until we continued to follow the way it was taking us before. By following the meters interference trail, we eventually ended up in one of the open aired stables and decided to stay there for a while as the meter seemed to be responding to a lot of the questions that we were asking. Whilst this was going on, we had securely placed the small ball on a stone ledge within the room. Several times throughout the following five minutes or so the ball began to flash, letting us know that it had been moved. Although the area has no roof and is open to the elements, we had already commented by this point on how calm it had seemed, with next to no wind blowing. This helped us eliminate the possibility that the ball had been moved by a breeze or a draught. Of course, there is always the possibility that the ball may had moved because we had not secured it sufficiently, despite thinking that we had. However, after replacing it several times, and securing it each time, I find it hard to believe that we had failed to do so consecutively, leading me to believe that the interference may have been caused by spirit activity.

An investigation that we carried out at Gresley Old Hall in Derbyshire gave us an interesting experience where interference with the equipment occurred, or in this instance, did not occur. We set up some EMF generators in a room, the idea being to flood the room with plenty of EMF and then see if it helped increase the activity within the room. Once the equipment was switched on and working, we were scanning the frequencies to see if we could hear anything on them. We also had an EMF meter primed and ready to detect anything, as well as a REM pod switched on to alert us to any activity. We ran the experiment for around fifteen minutes or so and were very disappointed when nothing seemed to be happening. Even the EMF meter was giving no results. Eventually, we ended the experiment and switched off the equipment. Once we did so, the EMF meter and REM pod became active and started to flash and bleep, alerting us to some form of activity. Some of the group even reported hearing footsteps in the room at the same time.

What I find so interesting about this is that it does help back up my theory that these spirits are operating on frequencies. The feeling that I got from this experiment is that when we were flooding the room with EMF, we had essentially blocked any spirits from interacting with us. Imagine that you are at a party and the kitchen is rather crowded, so you leave it a while and go back later. That is how I imagine the spirits had felt during this scenario. As soon as we had switched off the equipment and emptied the room of the EMF that we had been flooding it with, activity increased, almost as if the spirits had room now to enter the room and begin interacting with us again.

As mentioned at the start of this chapter, items being moved could also fall into the physical category, but I tend to only put experiences into the physical category if the moving items are done so in an aggressive manner towards an individual. There are plenty of examples that show how items can be moved in a more benign manner, and therefore, in my opinion, should fall into the interference category instead.

Some of these experiences might include seeing a trigger item move, either with your own eyes or with a video camera that you have set up on the object. For those of you who are unsure of what a trigger item is, it is when an object is placed somewhere in your chosen location in an effort to entice the spirit into moving it so that you may capture the movement as evidence. The trigger object itself can vary, depending on what or who you are interacting with. For example, if there are known to be the spirits of children in the location that you are investigating, then you may choose to use a teddy bear or a small toy. Another good idea is to place the trigger object in a tray of some sorts, something similar to a baking tray would work, and dust the bottom of the tray with talcum powder. Doing this will allow you to see if the item has moved at all just in case the movement isn't picked up on your recording device. There are also times, if it is easy to do so, where we will draw around an item in pencil, which allows us to see any movement when we go to check on the object periodically throughout the investigation.

There may also be examples of everyday household items being interfered with. I get to hear a lot of experiences when I am out on the road presenting to groups. Quite often an audience member will approach me before my presentation begins, or they will wait until I have finished speaking, to tell me about their experiences. Some of these people have never been on a paranormal investigation, so their experiences will come as part of everyday life. Unfortunately, a lot of people tend to miss or ignore the events that can occur daily because they are too busy, or they are sceptics and are not open to anything paranormal happening. Also, I find that if they are inexperienced in understanding what they are seeing, from a paranormal perspective, then their experiences are often misunderstood or missed entirely. Some of the experiences I have been told of range from doors that open and close by themselves, certain valuables, such as jewellery, being moved locations, electrical devices being manipulated, and even kitchen cupboard doors slamming in the night.

With all of the examples given above, including the trigger object, there are always possibilities of natural interference occurring, and the experience not being paranormal. With the opening and closing of doors, always ensure that there isn't a window open or a draught in the area that could be causing the door to slam or move. If items are being moved around the house, there is always a possibility of it being a child or someone else that you are living with either playing a game, trying to scare you, or genuinely moving it for a reason unknown to you. It is always worth checking with everyone in the house that this isn't the case. If it continues to occur, despite no one owning up to the activity, then you might consider setting up a camera to film the object in question and treat it as a trigger object. This could also work for the moving door activity. Doing this could help you prove once and for all that it is either spirit activity, or maybe it is a mischievous family member after all.

There was a really funny incident that occurred on one of our investigations a while back. We were investigating a private house and had set up trigger objects in several rooms, one being a small teddy bear that we had placed on a chair. When we came back to the trigger object to check on it the first time, we noticed that it had fallen off the chair and was found on the floor. This then happened the following three times that we had come to check on the object. It wasn't until we were analysing the video footage after the investigation that we noticed that the cause of movement had been the family cat. The cat had been jumping onto the chair and knocking the teddy bear off in the process. The teddy bear was clearly sitting in the family pet's favourite place. This just goes to show that filming your trigger objects is extremely important and that not every interference is paranormal.

A fellow investigator joined us at one of our recent investigations that we conducted at a local cemetery. One of the areas we focused on was the church itself and the large wooden door that is at the bottom of several stone steps. During the investigation, Les told us of the time that he had previously visited the same cemetery and had decided to see if he could get the spirits to interact with him by returning a stone that he had thrown down the steps. Imagine his surprise when a stone was actually returned to him, but up the steps. Now, this is a fascinating experience because had it been the other way around, it would have been rather easy to debunk. You could say that the stone that had been originally thrown by Les up the steps could easily have fallen back down towards him by way of gravity, rather than a playful spirit. However, the fact that the stone is returned up the steps, denying physics, really makes this experience stand out.

Whilst writing this book, I have been contacted by someone who has asked if we will visit their home to help them understand the activity that they are currently experiencing there. From what I have been told already, the person in question has had several traumatic experiences in their life, and one of them very recently. I am wondering, without having been to the location yet, if the traumatic events are a trigger for the activity that they are experiencing.

So far, I have seen one video that they have been kind enough to send to me. The video shows the individual placing a small ball, which they have told me is a children's toy, on the top of their kitchen work surface. For several seconds, the ball remains totally still, until the person asks for the ball to come towards them. Upon issuing that request, the ball does indeed begin to roll towards them and off the kitchen surface. One thing I have noticed is the peculiar movement of the ball as it begins to roll towards the camera. It doesn't seem to roll smoothly, as you would expect a ball to do. The movement seems rather staggered, and the ball seems hesitant in its movement. After the ball has rolled off the kitchen surface for the first time, the individual places it back on there and makes the same request. At this point the ball begins to move towards them again. It is a short video and that is all it shows, but the contents of the video footage have certainly intrigued me. When we do get to investigate the property, I will be making sure that there aren't any other reasons that the ball could have moved in the way that it has on the video footage. One thing that I will be checking is the kitchen surface and how level it is, ensuring that there isn't a slight slope that would have allowed gravity to cause the ball to roll towards the camera. The other possibility that has crossed my mind is the ball itself. With the item being a child's toy, it is possible that there is something inside the ball, either intended to rattle or make a sound when played with, or as a challenge to get out of the ball and put back in. The reason this has crossed my mind is because of the strange way in which the ball seems to move. The stuttered movement could be the result of the ball having an object inside it, causing it to move the way that it does. However, none of this would explain why the ball seems to be completely still one moment yet move towards the person as soon as they ask it to.

The traumatic experiences in this individual's life are something else that fascinate me. I do wonder if it is possible that when someone experiences a traumatic event or goes through some very difficult times in their life, they have an ability to manifest these types of experiences themselves. If we were to take the law of attraction theory and apply it to situations such as this, then you could theorise that going through negative situations and allowing that to impact in a negative way on your life will play a huge part in receiving negativity back. This is similar to what I have explained earlier in the book when discussing protection and how it could potentially all be psychological. Of course, if we were to take this theory far enough, we could even end up with the possibility that spirits are actually non-existent and are only the manifestation of each individual within the perception of their own reality.

This is something that has been at the forefront of my thoughts recently when researching the paranormal. More and more scientists are exploring the possibility that we do indeed live within a simulated reality or a holographic universe. If we apply this theory to the paranormal, then it certainly does open up a whole can of worms in regard to what the paranormal could actually be. If everything in the universe is a hologram, or a projection that is being created by the observer, as some mainstream scientists are now beginning to explore, then could it be that each paranormal experience could be the very same thing at its source, if only the hologram could be stripped away? So, every Bigfoot, spirit, UFO, or alien observed is ultimately created by the observer and is essentially the same point of attention, or piece of coding, behind the simulation, being manifested differently, depending on the experiencer.

Now, to take this theory a little further, what if the experience that is being manifested is only manifested in that particular way because of the beliefs and thoughts that are held within the mind of the experiencer. For example, if someone has a strong belief in Bigfoot, it stands to reason that they will encounter experiences that further that belief, similar to my earlier description of a believer in the Virgin Mary. This can also work the other way around, where those that have no belief or interest in the paranormal will never encounter an experience that may change their mind. So, when an individual tunes into a particular point of attention that is "paranormal" within the realms of our reality, they will only see what their subconscious wants them to see, which is ultimately whatever their beliefs are. Really, what we are seeing here, in its very basic form, is a behavioural pattern of humans simply finding evidence, or potentially manifesting it themselves, in order to back up their own belief system.

The house in Essex has been plagued by interference in their everyday lives for some time now. One of the main things that they experience is the throwing of pennies, which I will be going into in much more detail in the physical category chapter. When pennies aren't being thrown in anger at the family members, there are other interferences occurring, also. The entity that is residing there seems to enjoy nothing more than teasing the family and being mischievous. Sometimes, in other cases, a mischievous entity can be coped with and lived with, but in this instance the entity often takes it much further and becomes physical with the family members, as well as visitors to the house.

Whilst we were investigating the house, we had a camera set up at the top of the stairs where, I am sure by now you know, most of the activity seems to occur. The purpose of the camera was to have it focused on a trigger object experiment that we had set up, involving some pennies on a piece of paper that we had drawn around in order to make it easier to see if they had been interfered with. However, despite the pennies never moving throughout the entire investigation, the camera did capture some other good pieces of evidence. I have already mentioned the many orbs that were caught by this camera, and the opening door which followed the footsteps that we had heard, but it also caught something else that fascinated me when I watched the footage back. The camera captured something flashing on the floor of a bedroom. Upon closer inspection we realised that the flashing object was a video game controller. This particular controller is operated without a wire, similar to how a remote control would work for the television. The next time that you have your remote control in your hand, push a button on it and watch the control through your phone camera. When you do this, you can see the infrared that is transmitted by your remote control in order to control your television. This a great example of how we can only see a tiny fraction of the world around us, but we can certainly help ourselves see outside of our frequency range with the right pieces of equipment, just like when we are investigating the paranormal. Just like with the television remote, the video game controller has to have a button pressed in order for the infrared to transmit. What fascinated me the most about this particular piece of evidence was that the controller was simply lying on the floor, with nothing near it that could have been pressing the buttons. Despite this, the infrared light was flashing repeatedly for a couple of minutes. I did look at the controller closer to see if there could have been a fault with it, or to see if the buttons were sticking in, which could have caused the continuous flashing of the infrared, but nothing seemed to be wrong with the controller at all. I even asked the family if the controller was used regularly without any problems, and they confirmed that it was, and that they had never had any issues with it when using it to play video games.

Due to the ongoing situation in the family home, they decided to purchase indoor CCTV and placed several cameras around the house in an attempt to pick up any evidence that they may otherwise have missed. For example, when they were out, or not in a particular room. In doing this, they have been able to capture some absolutely fantastic video footage, as well as audio footage, too.

One piece of footage involved Kelly coming out of the kitchen and walking into the living room. No one else was in the kitchen area at the time, yet behind her, as she leaves the kitchen and makes her way to the living room, a pile of folders can be seen being thrown on to the floor from on top of a shelf. The noise caught her attention, and she can be heard on the footage shouting out at the entity in frustration.

Around Christmas time, they were also having Christmas figurines and decorations being thrown and broken. This is just a small glimpse of what the family are having to deal with on a day-to-day basis.

However, one occurrence that the cameras managed to capture is, without doubt, one of the best pieces of paranormal footage that I have ever had the pleasure of witnessing. For those that have seen me give a presentation on this evidence, then you will know which piece of footage I am about to discuss. The footage in question seems to show children's pyjamas and slippers appear out of thin air before being thrown on to a pile of clothes that are lying on the landing floor. The camera that captured this footage is positioned at the end of the landing, in the corner of the ceiling. This is the same wall where the small shadow was seen darting from the bedroom to the bathroom before slamming the door. There is nothing behind the camera other than a wall, with two doors either side, one leading to the bathroom, the other leading to the main bedroom. The reason that I mention this is because there is no possible way that someone could have stood behind the camera in order to have thrown the items of clothing on to the floor. There is no physical room for anyone, no matter how skinny, to fit behind the camera and not be seen. We did try to recreate this when we visited the house by making the thinnest member of our group stand with his back pressed up against the wall as much as possible, reach up with his arm and throw the items down. The camera managed to pick him up carrying out his actions and further proved to us that this could not have been carried out by a member of the family.

The cameras that the family installed were motion sensor cameras, which is great because it saves someone having to sit through hours of footage with nothing happening. What this does mean, however, is that it misses the very first second, if not less, of the movement before it switches on and begins to capture the activity. In the instance of the magically appearing clothing, the camera begins to film just as they come in to view. This is important to note, because the camera may have missed crucial evidence in helping us understand how this could have happened from a non-paranormal perspective. However, if someone was responsible for this, and I firmly believe that they were not, then the camera would have picked up their movements as they prepared to throw the clothing on to the floor, as proven with our efforts in trying to recreate the footage.

Also, this occurred in the middle of the night, with the family asleep downstairs. They had taken to sleeping downstairs during the height of the activity as they felt that it was the safest place to be. To make this footage even more interesting, if that is possible, is that Kelly claimed that the very same items that can be seen materialising out of thin air were, in fact, downstairs before the event occurred. This means that not only did the clothing appear out of nowhere and get thrown down on to the landing floor, but they were taken from downstairs in order to do so.

As I have already mentioned, this is one of the best pieces of footage that I have ever seen and having done everything I can to try and disprove it and having watched the footage more times than I can remember, I am convinced that there was no foul play going on here and that we have actually managed to capture something paranormal happening. For anyone that wishes to see this footage for themselves, my contact details are at the back of the book and I would be more than happy to share with you. The same can be said for any of the footage that I have described throughout this book.

Category Five: Empathetic Experiences

In a similar fashion to a sensory experience, an empathetic experience can be an extremely personal one, and can even leave an emotional mark on the experiencer. A sensory and empathetic experience can be very closely linked, but empathetic does differ due to the experience being something that is linked to a spirit's past or the history of a location, where the experiencer can re-live a particular emotion or event, which may then turn into a sensory experience.

Every location that you have visited, and will visit in the future, will have a history. Even if the building itself is relatively new, the location that the building has been erected on will have been the place of many historical goings on. It is these goings on that may have etched themselves into the fabric of the building or location and could then be transferred to an experiencer by way of an empathetic experience.

As alluded to above, an empathetic experience can come in a multitude of guises. It could be that you begin to feel a pain in a particular part of your body when in a certain area of the location that then vanishes when you move onto the next area. It could also manifest itself as a certain emotion. Becoming overwhelmed with sadness, anger, or happiness, which is an emotion more common than it is given credit for. Walking into a certain part of a location could trigger one of these emotions which can appear suddenly and, no matter what you do to suppress it, can stay with you for quite some time.

When it comes to equipment and capturing empathetic experiences, it can be almost impossible. This type of experience is such a personal one, that most equipment becomes redundant when being used to try and capture, or prove, an empathetic experience. One thing that you could do is to try and focus on the surroundings of the individual during the occurrence.

For example, you could check to see if the temperature has changed around them, or even if their temperature has changed at all. This can be done using a laser temperature gun or, if possible, an infrared thermal imaging camera, to see any increase or decrease in their bodily temperature. Also, try and film them whilst the experience is happening. Being able to look back at the video footage and analyse their body language may help to understand how they were feeling against what they were saying at the time. Not only this, but you never know what you may capture on the footage. A shadow lurking behind the person, near to them, or actually interacting with them, could help to prove that they were truly experiencing something paranormal. Items such as EMF meters or REM pods could also be utilised in this type of situation. Any interference that they may show during the incident, could again help to prove that there was actually something going on, especially if these items were inactive prior to the experience.

One thing that I try my best not to do, particularly when visiting a new location that we haven't investigated previously, is to find out anything about the building or area of the location. There are several reasons for this, but the main reason is because I do not want any knowledge, even if it is stored inside my subconscious, to come through when investigating. In my opinion, this can give the illusion of an empathetic experience and may trick you into thinking that you are experiencing something that is directly related to the location. Of course, this becomes much more difficult once you have visited the same location multiple times, as you will slowly become used to it and no doubt learn more about it with each visit that you make.

Psychologically speaking, it would be very easy for a sceptic to dismiss the claims of an empathetic experience should the individual claiming to have had the experience already know about the location, area or history that may have had a hand in helping to form their experience. Imagine a scenario where a group of people are being shown around a location as part of an investigation. Whilst on the tour, one of the guides decides to stop the group in a particular area and point out that where they had stopped was the precise area of a tragic accident that had occurred decades before. Unfortunately, someone had lost their life in that very area when the roof had caved in, subsequently crushing the victim, and suffocating them. As this story is being told, a member of the group raises their hand and tells the guide that it is interesting they should say what they had as it just so happened that since the group had stopped in this area, they had been having difficulty breathing and felt as though something was crushing their chest. Now, the sceptic in me would question this experience. On the face of it, it is a classic empathetic experience. The individual is picking up on an emotion or a feeling that was felt by someone during a traumatic event and is replaying those feelings and emotions through themselves. However, you do have to ask the question; would this person have been feeling anything at all should the guide not have said anything in regard to the accident that had occurred there previously? In my opinion, the answer to that questions would be no. Interestingly, this very same scenario actually did happen on a public investigation I was participating in a few years back. At the time, I remember thinking that the only reason that the individual had picked up on those feelings is because the guide had almost told them to feel that way. I also remember thinking how it was bad form on behalf of the guide for telling the group the history of the location prior to the investigation getting fully under way. I have absolutely no problems with telling any of the guests about the history of a location should they ask, but should they enquire before or during the investigation, I do tend to tell them to wait until the end of the event and I will answer any questions that they should have then. The reason for this is because I do not wish to plant any potential spoilers in their mind that may come back and present themselves under the guise of a paranormal experience at some point later in the investigation.

Now let us alter that true scenario a little. Imagine the group had stopped and the guide had told the group that they were just going to stop a while and do some calling out or some listening. During this brief session, a member of the group lets the others know that they are really struggling to breathe and feel as though something is pressing down on their chest. The guide sees to their safety and ensures that they are feeling well enough to continue before the group finally move on with their tour and the investigation gets fully underway. A little while later, or maybe at the end of the event, one of the guides pulls the previously affected group member to one side and lets them know that the area where they had reported the sense of breathlessness and a crushing sensation was the very same area where the roof had collapsed and crushed someone decades before.

Putting these two scenarios side by side, even if you are not a sceptic, you have to admit that one of them is not only more believable, but also more ethical from the perspective of the guide. There is every possibility that the first scenario had only occurred due to the supposedly affected individual being subconsciously manipulated to feel the way that they did. The second scenario allowed that person to feel the atmosphere, the energy, and the history themselves and somehow draw a conclusion that was both fascinating and historically accurate.

This particular form of subconscious manipulation, whether it be deliberate, which can unfortunately be the case, or not, is one of the most common reasons for empathetic experiences to occur. It is a similar situation to when one of the group members calls out that they are feeling cold or that they feel as though they are being watched. Just one person calling this out can hugely impact the rest of the group and can, more often than not, create the same feeling for others, too, despite them not having been feeling this way prior to hearing that someone else was. Sadly, it really can be this easy to feel that you have had a paranormal experience, when in fact, it is just the power of suggestion.

With that being said, I do find it very interesting when someone encounters an empathetic experience that may allow them to have a better understanding of the location's history, despite having had no previous knowledge of the place or its back story. When this occurs, and it does happen regularly, I cannot help but think that there is something out of the ordinary going on. Whether it is a spirit lending a hand in helping someone understand a moment in their life or whether it is some kind of psychic ability that it completely unrelated to spirits, I am not entirely sure, but either possibility is a fascinating one. If it isn't a spirit that is responsible for the individual's experience, then there may be some kind of psychic activity at play. Either possibility is as fascinating as the other.

A while ago we investigated a location known as Whittington Castle in Oswestry, near the English and Welsh border. This particular location offers the possibility to investigate both inside as well as outside, around parts of the ruins. As mentioned previously, there are always potential issues when investigating outside. Of course, there are issues with investigating inside, too, but I find that there are more external influences that can affect an investigation when outside, such as weather, people, animals, and cars to name a few.

Whilst we were investigating an inside area, we had two amazing empathetic experiences, one involving myself. As you know, researching a location previously is not something that I tend to do, and, sticking to this, I knew absolutely nothing about this location prior to our arrival. Both of the experiences occurred in the same area, a room that is now used to conduct wedding ceremonies. The room was rectangular in shape with chairs placed around the outside. At one end of the room was a kind of alter where the bride and groom would be placed during a ceremony. At one point, whilst we were in this room, I was sat on one of the chairs at the opposite end of the room to where the alter is. For the entire time that I was sat there, which was around five minutes or so, I felt an unnerving feeling that I just could not shake off. I remember the feeling extremely nervous, bouncing my legs up and down and rubbing my sweaty hands together. It must have been noticeable as another member of the group, who was sat a few chairs away from me, moved closer to see how I was feeling. I remember telling them that I was very nervous, and I felt as though I was awaiting some potentially bad news, similar to how you might feel the morning of receiving your exam results. They suggested that I should stand up and have a walk around to see if that might help. I told them that I felt that standing up would only bring this unwanted news quicker. Eventually, though, unable to take the feeling anymore I did stand up and had a walk towards the other end of the room. As I approached the alter the previous feeling of nerves and trepidation vanished. Now that I felt more comfortable, I decided to take a seat in the corner of the room, near to the alter. Our guide for the night was sat nearby. They weren't participating in any of our sessions but were simply there for our safety and to unlock and lock areas as we came and went. During the short time I was sat in this chair I had an overwhelming sense of power. I remember feeling that I was above every other person in the room and that they should all bow down before me. I whispered that I was feeling this way to the guide who pointed towards the floor around ten feet in front of us. When I looked to see what it was that she was pointing out to me I noticed one of the group had knelt down on one knee, facing where we were sat. I called out to them and asked why they were kneeling down, and they stated that they just felt like it was the right thing to do. At the end of the investigation, the guide approached me and told me a little bit more about that particular room. Many, many years ago, that room had been used by the local lord for his court, where he would settle disputes with the locals and hand out any rewards or punishment. The one end of the room, where I was feeling anxious and nervous, is where people would wait to be called in front of the lord. The other end of the room, where I felt very powerful is where the lord would sit during his sessions. When I heard this from the guide I was in utter shock. I had never really experienced anything like this previously and it took a while for me to get my head around what had happened. I had been picking up on the history of the room and had been playing out, emotionally, what had previously occurred in that room. It was only whilst I was driving home after the investigation had finished that I remembered the one member of the group who had been kneeling in front of where I was sat, mimicking what a person would have done when called in front of their lord. To me, this just further confirmed that I had indeed been part of an empathetic experience and had been reliving the history and emotions of that room.

During the same investigation, in the very same room, whilst I was having my own personal experience, another member of the group was also going through an empathetic experience of their own. Whilst stood in the middle of the room, they began to have a severe pain in their midriff. The pain was so extreme at one point that they had doubled up with the agony. They likened the pain to what it would have felt like should they had been shot. My initial thought when I heard about this later in the evening was that they were possibly feeling the effects of someone who had been shot with an arrow, given the timeframe of the location. However, the guide later told us that only a few decades previously, a man had been rushed in off the street and into the same room with a burst appendix. When that knowledge is revealed, you just cannot help being shocked at the comparison between what the member of the group had been feeling and what the man decades before would have felt. Just like I had, they were experiencing the history of the location empathetically.

Another investigation that we carried out at a location in Wolverhampton provided another great example of an empathetic experience. This experience was much darker than the previous one that I have just described. A handful of us were conducting a calling out session in one of the bedrooms. The room contained three single beds and a small vanity table with a stool. Besides this, there was not much room for moving around, so everyone had taken a seat, my seat being the stool. One person decided not to sit down, however, and was pacing nervously from one end of the room to the next, with some difficulty due to the lack of space. Eventually, I asked them what was wrong and if they cared to take a seat, offering them a spot on the bed near to me. They stated that they felt as though they should not be sitting on the bed. As the only other option was the stool, I offered to give them the stool and I would sit on the bed. They eventually accepted the offer and I moved to the bed. Within seconds of sitting down on the bed I was overcome with the most severe hopelessness and sadness. I had never, and have never since, felt such raw emotion and a willingness to end my own life. The feeling was so strong that I remember saying to the person next to me that if I were to be offered a gun there and then, I would take it and use it, no question. I could not stop sobbing and it felt like the feeling would never cease. Whilst this was manifesting, someone that was sat near to the door lifted the latch and opened it slightly. When asked why she had done that, she said that she felt like the door had to be open and to have it closed wasn't a good thing. Due to my emotional state, I removed myself from the room and took five minutes outside trying to regather myself. Finally, the experience passed, and I began to feel like my normal self. A few days after the investigation, we were doing some research on the place only to find that there had been claims of sexual abuse involving young children having happened in the very room that this experience had occurred. I have absolutely no doubt that sitting on the very bed that these vile acts were carried out on triggered an empathetic experience unlike any that I have ever had before or will ever have again. The hopelessness and grief that I was feeling was a retelling of the feelings that the poor children would have experienced. It also explains why the other member of the group had felt the need to open the bedroom door, as the door being closed could very well have signified that the horrendous acts were taking place, and the spirits would want the door open as a means of escape.

Category Six: Physical Experiences

For most people who investigate the paranormal, witnessing or capturing evidence that falls into the physical category is the ultimate piece of evidence that can then be used to prove that spirits exist. An empathetic experience or a sensory experience is very personal, as I believe all experiences to be to some extent, but a physical experience is something that can be witnessed by multiple people, recorded, or captured on a photograph and shown to others to prove what you have encountered.

As with all categories, there is a cross over between the physical and others, particularly sensory, where feeling a touch could fall into the physical category. However, in my opinion it is fully dependent on the type of touch that is felt. A gentle tap on the arm or a soft touch is very different to being pushed and pulled around in an aggressive manner. Just like seeing things move can fall into an interference category, if an item is deliberately thrown at you or moved in an aggressive way, then I would be inclined to categorise it within the physical experiences.

One of the positives about physical experiences is that the majority of them can be captured using standard pieces of equipment, without having to spend too much money. Video cameras can be used to capture objects being thrown or to witness someone being shoved or attacked. Cameras can be used to photograph scratches or other marks that someone may have received seemingly from nowhere. Of course, as with all experiences, the best piece of equipment is the experiencer themselves.

We have already covered items being moved in the interference category, but there are times that objects may move in a more hostile way, namely when the objects are launched in your general direction. When something like this happens, it is very easy to panic and automatically assume that the movement was caused by a spirit. The issue with moving objects in the physical category is that it can become increasingly difficult to try and debunk a moving object when it has been thrown at speed across a large distance. Items moving in a benign manner, as discussed in the interference chapter, can be easier to solve. It may be a slightly uneven surface that has caused the object to move, or a family pet may have moved the item, as previously discussed. However, when something hits you and it has clearly been thrown aggressively, then blaming something such as a draft, a breeze or an uneven surface just doesn't seem to hold up very well as a reason for such activity. One thing you could consider is that if an object has fallen from a height, then gravity could give the illusion that it has been thrown with force. For me, the only other logical explanation would be either a member of the group has thrown the object, or it is the actions of a mischievous individual that happens to be in the same vicinity as you whilst you are investigating, and they wish to disturb you. It is extremely difficult to try and comprehend that the actions could be that of your own group. As I have mentioned previously, it always counts to surround yourself with a team that you can trust fully. If you ever find yourself on a public event, with people that you have met for the first time that night, then it is important to ensure that any evidence you capture, whether that be flying objects or of the audible kind, is analysed as soon as possible, as there is every possible chance that it could be someone within the group who is not taking the event as seriously as you are. I understand that this may come across as rather negative and untrusting, but having had these experiences myself, I cannot stress enough how frustrating it can be to believe that you have captured or experienced a great paranormal occurrence, only to find that it was falsified by someone nearby.

One of my earliest recollections of having objects thrown at me goes back to my very first paranormal investigation at Dudley Castle. It was a largely uneventful event, if I am being honest, with the very few moments of interest coming from the group medium that was there. This was a public event that I had paid to attend, and it certainly opened my eyes as to how some of these events are carried out. I have described in my previous book my thoughts on certain franchised groups, along with the entertainment shows on television, and their impact on the investigative field, particularly where grass roots investigators and researchers are concerned.

The resident medium ensured that most people left the event having the sense of encountering something paranormal, even if they hadn't. Unfortunately, this is a common theme with certain groups and not one that I am a fan of. Eventually, towards the end of the investigation, we were allowed some time to wander off and conduct some independent investigating, which was something I jumped at the chance to do. Being local to Dudley Castle, I was very familiar with the layout of the location and had already pinpointed particular areas that I wished to spend some time in. One of those areas was a part of the castle that had been turned into a walk-through museum, which was a really interesting part of the castle during opening hours. However, during the investigation, in the early hours of the morning, it wasn't so welcoming. The room that my wife and I settled in was a large, round room. The walls were stone, as it was inside the castle, and there was a stone ledge on the circular wall that we decided to sit on. In the middle of the room there was a display that depicted how the castle might have looked hundreds of years ago. Once we were settled, we decided to do some calling out. My wife is a sceptic but had accompanied me as it was my birthday present from her. As we were calling out, we began to hear what sounded like a window being tapped lightly. I stood up and began to shine my torch around the room trying to find out where the noise could possibly be coming from, particularly as there were no windows in the room. We then realised that the display in the centre of the room was inside a glass case. Sitting back down, I began to call out again, this time asking for the spirits to make the same noise they had previously, whilst now focusing on the display. Within around a minute or so of asking, we heard the noise again, twice. The second time that we heard the noise it was followed very quickly by what sounded like a stone bouncing across the floor. When I shone my torch onto the ground, it was difficult to confirm what we originally thought due to the fact that the ground had plenty of small pieces of gravel and stones littered about, carried in from outside. At this point I decided to play the spirit at its own game and threw a small piece of gravel across the room so that it hit the wall. The noise it made as it scattered across the floor was the exact same noise that we had heard moments before. Just as I threw the piece of gravel, I called out for the spirit to throw it back to me. Around half a minute later we heard the now familiar sound of the glass being tapped, followed by the sound of the gravel bouncing across the floor. This time, though, the gravel hit my shoe. Once again, I threw it back across the room and asked for the spirit to throw it back, and sure enough, the gravel came back, bouncing off the glass display in the centre of the room and this time hitting me on the arm. This time, however, it didn't wait for me to throw the gravel back before another piece was thrown, hitting my wife on the chest. At this point, we decided to leave the room as we began to feel very unnerved with the way the events were unfolding, seemingly increasing in activity involving objects being thrown at us. Once outside, I asked my wife what she had made of the experience and, in true sceptic fashion, she said that it could very easily have been someone else in the adjacent room tricking us into thinking we were interacting with a spirit. Despite her scepticism, I believe it was fantastic experience. To have items thrown at you may not be a nice situation to be in, but we had left the area before it could have potentially taken a nasty turn.

Just across the road from Dudley Castle sits a very famous hotel, known nationally for its spirit activity. It was propelled into its popularity due to a particular television programme investigating there. The Station Hotel is a fantastic location, offering paranormal investigative teams the chance to investigate some of its guest rooms, as well as the cellars. Having investigated there a couple of times, I can certainly see why it has earned such popularity amongst the paranormal community. However, it wasn't during a paranormal event that I encountered the following experience. The hotel, building on the acclaim that it has gathered, also holds special evenings where guests can enjoy a meal followed by an audience with a medium. They also hold clairvoyance nights, as well as many other events similar in nature.

Once again, as a gift from my wife, I was treated to one of the events where a medium would perform in front of a small crowd. Once we had finished our meal, we all congregated in the bar area whilst the room was rearranged and made ready for the next part of the evening. During this brief intermission, I made my way to the bar to buy a couple of drinks. There weren't many people at the bar, but I had to wait whilst the barman was serving someone. It was whilst I was waiting that I witnessed a pint glass fly off the shelf above the bar and smash against the back wall, just above the cash register. Most of the people in the bar at that time had heard the glass smash but had assumed that the glass had been dropped by a member of staff. I caught the barman's eye, who was pouring a drink at the time, and asked him if he had just seen what I had seen. He confirmed that he had and that it was about the fourth time that it had happened that week. I was in shock. It was the first time that I had witnessed such activity. I asked the barman if he minded me taking a closer look. He nodded and I made my way behind the bar. Upon closer inspection, the whole experience was made all the stranger because I noticed that the shelf that the glass had flown off, which was above the bar, was actually designed so that it sloped downwards, a design made to prevent the glasses from sliding off in error and potentially injuring a member of staff behind the bar. This made the experience incredibly difficult to debunk as my original thoughts were that the glass had been wet and had simply slipped off the shelf. This was clearly not the case for two reasons. The first being that the shelf sloped away, preventing the glass from just sliding off, unless the barman had placed it right on the edge. The second reason also eliminates that possibility because not only did the glass fall of the shelf, but it also propelled itself the depth of the bar, which is roughly six feet or so, and smashed against the back wall. If the glass had been unbalanced on the edge of the shelf then I could see that as being the reason it had fallen off, but it does not account for the fact that the glass flew six feet into the back wall at speed and smashed. I was left with the sense that what I had just seen was certainly paranormal.

Some of the best physical experiences that I have personally encountered occurred whilst we were investigating the family home in Essex. During our investigation there, we decided that it would be best to put a person in each room of the house. The reason for this was because the entity that is residing there seemed to be moving from room to room, always one step ahead of us. The first room that I was given was a bedroom belonging to one of the teenagers. The bed seemed to take up most of the room, so there wasn't much room left for moving around. As you walked through the door, the bed was on the left-hand side, which I decided to sit on whilst waiting to see if there would be any interaction. I was sat there for roughly five minutes when all of a sudden, I felt something hit me in the back. I instantly stood up and turned on my torch, seeing if I could see what it was that had hit me. As I shone the torch on the bed, I could just make out a small shape. As I got closer, I quickly realised that it was a trainer. At first, I was confused. Where had the trainer come from? Shining the torch around the room I noticed that hanging on the back of the bedroom door was a rack to put shoes into. My initial reaction was that the shoe must have fallen out and hit me, but this quickly left my mind because that would have been impossible. When sat on the bed, the door was to my right, roughly four feet or so in front of me. For the shoe to hit me how it did would mean that it was lifted out of the pouch on the back of the door, moving past me, before turning back on itself and hitting me in the back. I am sure that you will agree with me when I say that the very thought of that happening is impossible. What is stranger is that I didn't hear the shoe move whatsoever. In fact, I wasn't aware of anything until it struck me in the back. I left the room, leaving the shoe where it had landed on the bed, and made the rest of the group aware of what happened.

Several room swaps later, and another member of the group was now in that bedroom. After a few minutes of being in there alone, they came running out of the room, down the landing and into the bathroom, where I was stood, claiming that something had hit them in the back. We gathered in the bedroom with our torches to see what we could find. As soon as we entered the bedroom our torches shone upon the trainer, now lying in the middle of the floor. I turned to the bed and noticed that the trainer I had left there had gone. The very same trainer that had hit me in the back had now also hit another member of the group in their back. I asked them how they had been stood, or sat, in the room when it had happened. They stated that they had been stood with the bed to their right, facing the door. This means that the trainer would have had to lift from the bed, move around the back of them and turn in a right angle in order to hit them in their back. Again, an impossible maneuver for an inanimate object. The journey back from the house was around two hours, of which we spent a large amount of trying to figure out how the experiences could have happened without being paranormal. It is safe to say that we could not find any reasonable explanation to show how it could have happened and concluded that we had most certainly experienced paranormal activity.

One of the most common reports from the family in Essex was that of coins, predominantly pennies, being thrown around their home. I must add, though, that it isn't always a penny that is being thrown. They have previously had New Zealand coins being thrown, which is a country none of the family, or their friends, have ever visited. One of the very first videos that I was sent of the activity in the home showed Lee putting his work boots on, bending down to tie his laces and a penny being thrown over the top of him. I must admit that upon viewing the video for the first time, I was adamant that the coin had been thrown by Lee as a joke. This was until I witnessed the coin throwing first-hand, less than five minutes from entering the home. We were all gathered in the living room introducing ourselves to the family when we heard something hit the wall on the stairs. I turned to see what it was when a penny came bouncing into the living room. The floor downstairs is laminated so the sound of the coins bouncing along it are quite loud. I couldn't believe it. All of my previous doubts about who had been responsible for throwing the coins were dismissed straight away. There was no one else upstairs at that time.

A few moments later, one of the family members was sat on the bottom of the stairs listening to us talking in the living room. All of a sudden, a penny was launched from upstairs, bouncing off the back wall, over their head where they were sat and, again, rolled towards us in the living room. We have this particular penny being thrown caught on camera. As the penny hits the back wall, the person sitting on the stairs visibly panics and runs into the living room where the rest of us were stood. I have studied this video and, knowing that there is no one upstairs, there is no way that this could have been carried out by anyone in the house, including the family member who was sat on the stairs at the time.

Interestingly, if you are wondering how hard these coins are being thrown, then there are photographs that show the indentations in the wall from where the coins have left their mark. One of these photographs shows how the plaster on the wall has been chipped away by the coin hitting it, such was the force of the contact. The other thing I find very strange about these photographs is that the indentations are fully round. If a coin were to be thrown against a wall and leave a mark, I would expect that the edge of the coin would hit the wall and leave a mark in the shape of a line, where the edge of the coin had made contact. However, this does not seem to be the case with these photos. They show that the coin has struck the wall whole, leaving a perfectly round mark, in some cases. This seems almost impossible to me, as the chances of the coin striking the wall in such a way even once seems extremely unlikely, never mind the several times that it has been caught on separate pictures.

One of the best coin throwing experiences that the family managed to capture on video footage involved the landing area. As I have mentioned previously, the landing area and the stairs seem to be the most active area of the house. You will notice that most of the activity I have described throughout this book involves these areas. This video starts with Lee moving across the landing, his movement having triggered the motion sensor camera. You hear one of the young children shout from downstairs asking if the penny that had just been thrown, prior to the camera beginning to film, had been thrown by Lee. He shouts down that it was, despite it not being him at all. When I asked him about this, he said that it was because they try their best to not let the children know what is going on, for obvious reasons. Lee's response seems to satisfy the child and he begins to get ready to go down the stairs, whilst muttering under his breath about how the entity shouldn't start anything as they were on their way out. As he approaches the top of the stairs and begins to walk down them, a coin is thrown against one of the bedroom doors, with an audibly loud bang, before landing on the floor. The reason I like this footage so much is because it is one of the very few where you can actually see the coin land after it has been thrown. Just after you hear the coin hit the door, it appears on the carpeted landing. This happened right after Lee had asked for nothing else to happen, almost as if the action was done to irritate him as much as possible and claim that Lee had no authority over whatever this entity wishes to do.

The last example of a coin being thrown that I will give, though there are plenty more that we have managed to capture on video, involves a family friend visiting the home and coming under fire from a penny being thrown at him. The footage shows the family friend entering the house and walking towards the kitchen, which is located at the back of the house. To get there, however, he had to pass the foot of the stairs, which by now you will know is the epicentre of activity within the home. Just as he passes by the foot of the stairs, a coin is visibly thrown from up the stairs, bouncing off the back wall and lands at his feet. The visitor is clearly shocked and cannot believe what he has just witnessed. As the experience happens, Lee comes out of the kitchen and tells the visitor that it could be because he had just had a go at the entity. What is interesting here is that the entity really does seem to react to being told what it can and cannot do. It doesn't seem to enjoy being told off or being scolded for its actions. I believe that this is why it tends to attack Lee so much, as Lee is the man of the house, and the entity may see him as a threat to its dominance within the home. Although it does target the other members of the family, Lee most certainly seems to get the brunt of it.

It is difficult to tell with this video if there was anyone else up the stairs at the time that the penny is thrown at the visitor. The family claim that there was not, and I am inclined to believe them. Having been there myself and having experienced on multiple occasions exactly what this visitor experienced makes me believe that this footage is another fantastic example of physical paranormal activity.

What is interesting about all of these coins that are being thrown around the home is that there seems to be an endless supply of them. After a while, the family began to keep all of the coins that have been thrown in a glass jar by way of ensuring they cannot be used again. The family have even conducted their own little experiment where they counted the number of coins that they had collected in a jar and were confident, after looking around the house, that there were no more that could be thrown. Despite this, more coins were still appearing. When they did, they once again counted the number of coins in their glass jar only to find that the number was the same as it had been previously, meaning that these extra coins had seemed to literally be manifesting from nowhere. This seems like an impossible feat, but when you consider the incident involving the clothes that had manifested out of nowhere, as described previously, and the fact that they are having foreign coins being used, it certainly goes a long way to backing up the theory that these coins are not originally from the house.

Being touched by a paranormal entity can come as part of the sensory category, but when that contact seems to be more violent in nature, then I would not hesitate in placing the experience within the physical category. There have been plenty of times that we have been on an investigation with both the group and the public and there have been claims of being shoved, pushed, and pulled about by some unseen force. Being pushed around by an unseen force is an incredibly frightening experience and can leave an individual feeling vulnerable and helpless. It may seem strange, but I genuinely believe that you can tell whether the contact is benign or malicious in nature by the experience itself. Having been on the receiving end of both of these types of experiences and having researched many cases that involve both a sensory type of touch and a more aggressive, physical touch, it is easy to see that spirits are capable of both.

I have even experienced this myself, many times. In my previous book, I go into detail describing a human pendulum experiment that I participated in at Drakelow Tunnels. It involved me being hit on the forehead and propelled backwards.

Luckily, there was someone at hand to catch me before I hit the floor, but for minutes following the experience I was extremely dazed and confused, with the feeling of a vice like grip persisting on my forehead. Such was my confusion following the experience that I even briefly forgot what day of the week it was. It was an experience that has stayed with me to this day.

Some of the categories that I have mentioned throughout this book could very well be psychological and be occurring in the mind of the experiencer, whether they know it is or not. Take sensory, for example, where smelling experiences can occur. This could most certainly be within the mind of the individual experiencing the smell and may not be paranormal at all. However, there is no real way of knowing. If the experiencer claims that they can smell something, we have to place our trust in that person. A physical type of contact, however, is far more, well, physical. We are led to believe that we live in a physical world, although I would argue differently. There have been many times that I have heard people claim that they cannot believe in the paranormal because they can only put their faith and trust into something that they can see and feel. Well, it doesn't get much closer to that than when you are physically moved around by something that you cannot explain. With that being said, though, there are times that this type of experience could be considered to be not paranormal in nature. As you should know by now, I always consider other options when experiencing or viewing paranormal activity, to the point that I have even been accused of being a complete sceptic and asked why I even bother researching the paranormal at all. The answer to this is simple; I do believe in the paranormal, but also believe that the human mind is capable of creating paranormal experiences where there are none at all. Pareidolia, for example. The fact that such a thing as pareidolia even exists means that all paranormal experiences need to be scrutinised before they can be confirmed as paranormal, and even then, there could still be doubts. How can you not believe in the paranormal and in entities and energies existing around us once you understand that there is so much around us that we cannot interact with?

I have been on investigations that have areas where the people are quite close together due to the size of the room. This can be a cause for believing that you have experienced physical contact, when in fact it is just the person next to you shuffling around and catching you with their elbow or treading on your foot. There is always something to consider not just with physical contact, but with all paranormal activity. However, as I have already mentioned, it is rather more difficult to debunk someone being attacked, shoved, punched, or prodded, particularly when it is happening in front of your own eyes, where the experiencer is reacting to the contact, yet you cannot see anything that could possibly be doing it.

An interesting video that I was sent by the family in Essex seemed to show Lee being attacked by an unseen force. Lee claimed that it felt like he had been punched in the head and the video certainly seems to show a reaction that would match his claim.

The footage show Lee making his way over to the bottom of the staircase and sitting down on the stairs, beginning to smoke a cigarette. He isn't even sat down for five seconds when his whole body is rocked to the side from a seemingly unseen attack. Instantly, he shoots to his feet and that is where the footage stops. This event didn't happen in the night, which is worrying for the family, as it occurred whilst people were moving around the house, going about their daily business. For example, just before Lee sits down, one of the teenagers runs up the stairs. For something like this to happen in the middle of a family home, with children playing in the background, is very concerning. I have studied this video numerous times. How easy, I originally thought, would it be to fake being punched and simply rock your head to one side to make it look as though it was real. This, however, doesn't seem to be as easy as I originally thought it would be. Lee's body language whilst being attacked is, in my opinion, congruent to that of someone that has just been punched whilst sat down. His one leg even shoots out as contact is made as if to steady himself. This would seem a minor detail for someone potentially looking to fake this type of experience to remember to do. Also, the way that he acts once attacked is interesting to watch. There is the briefest of moments where he doesn't seem to quite understand what has happened, but as soon as the realisation hits home, he shoots up just as the footage ends. One of the most fascinating aspects to this footage, apart from the fact that an individual is visibly being attacked by an unseen entity, is that the contact is actually heard on the video footage. The sounds comes across like a solid thud as soon as his head rocks to the side and his leg shoots out. It may just be that the noise is being made by the leg shooting out, but how? The leg doesn't make contact with anything in order to create a noise and it doesn't stamp down but lifts off the floor. Also, right before the attack actually occurs, Lee looks to his left, which is the side that the punch comes from, almost as if he has sensed that something is near him or sensed that something is about happen. Within a second of looking to his left, his body is rocked backwards by the unseen punch. In my opinion, this is more evidence that the entity feels threatened by Lee and is trying to assert its dominance over what it deems to be the leader of the family.

As I have already mentioned, these types of experiences, when captured on camera and not happening to yourself, are far more difficult to debunk. In these situations, it really is a case of having to place all of your trust in the experiencer that they are being truthful and honest about what has happened to them. Having spent time with the family and having experienced several events in the house myself, I have absolutely no reason to believe that they would falsify evidence and also cannot see any reason that they would feel the need to. They haven't used these experiences for their own benefit in any way, and when you see and hear how scared the young children are, it would take a very cynical person to believe that they are faking the haunting.

Epilogue

As stated in the introduction, the purpose of this book was to take the beginners of the paranormal investigative field, who have read my previous book, onwards in their journey of research. I hope that it has helped you further understand the type of experiences that you may encounter now that you are out there investigating the paranormal. For those more seasoned investigators, hopefully the experiences that I have detailed throughout this book were of interest and maybe they have helped you understand how to categorise and deal with each experience as it happens.

Throughout this book I have given detailed experiences that have mostly been witnessed and experienced first-hand by myself as well as describing how best to capture those experiences and debunk them, if necessary. Where I wasn't the witness, I have described the experience as best as I possibly can using the witness and their recollections to ensure that it is as detailed and as truthful as possible.

Experiencing any paranormal event is as personal an experience as you can get. The very same experience will mean something completely different to different people. We can take as much equipment as we would like when out investigating, but the longer I have been researching the paranormal, the stronger I feel about our own bodies being the best piece of equipment that can be used. There are pieces of equipment that can be used in order to aid us when trying to interact with the energies that exist outside of our range of perception, which is where, in my opinion, these energies reside. For this reason, it is still important to use equipment when out investigating, but it is important to choose the equipment that you do use carefully. There are a lot of items out there that are being used, including mobile phone apps, that do nothing to truly capture paranormal experiences and evidence. My kit bag has shrunk considerably since I first started investigating the paranormal. For most of the investigations that I participate in now I tend to take a camera, a spirit board, and an EVP recorder. Occasionally, I may use a spirit box or REM pod, but on the whole, I really do use my own body to tune in to the surroundings and the energy. By doing this, you may be surprised at just how much you actually pick up and experience, instead of focusing all of your attention on screens and devices that can actually distract you from potential experiences.

I would like to end the book focusing on the future of evidence and whether it can ever truly be trusted again. With the ever-increasing usage of CGI, photoshop and other picture and video editing tools, will we ever truly be able to trust any evidence that is put in front of us in the future? There are always going to be difficulties when it comes to trying to convince the hard-nosed sceptics that are out there that what we term the paranormal is a reality. Besides asking them to just take our word for it that our experiences did actually occur and that there is a world out there full of spirits and other paranormal entities, the only other way we can work on convincing them is to show them solid proof. Proof that our experiences did manifest within this reality and that spirits do exist.

However, I am sure if you have collected evidence yourself and made the decision to show this evidence to the public, you will have come across certain individuals that have accused your evidence of being nothing but fake. I have had this happen many times before and, believe me, it doesn't get any easier to deal with. There are a multitude of emotions that you will encounter if and when someone dismisses the evidence that you believe to be so fantastic in proving the existence of the paranormal. You may feel anger or frustration towards the sceptic and struggle to understand how, despite looking at the same piece of evidence that you believe to be so truthful, they can still be so dismissive of the paranormal. There may also be an anger at the fact that they are potentially calling you a liar by stating that your evidence is either fake or doesn't prove anything. This can be particularly hurtful if the evidence that you are presenting was an experience that you had personally encountered yourself. You may also feel hopeless and question whether there is any point in collecting any evidence at all if all anyone is going to do is simply ignore any evidence that is put in front of them, no matter how convincing you believe that evidence to be.

Some people, no matter the evidence that is presented to them, will never believe in the paranormal. Having an understanding of this will benefit you in the long run, as the emotions that I have just described can be extremely disheartening if you expect everybody to view your evidence in the same way that you do. There are also the people that will claim that any evidence they see is fake or it is a forgery. They will blame CGI or claim that the picture or video footage is doctored to make it look authentic. However, it will help you to understand their viewpoint if you just put yourself in their position for a moment. Although it may not be something that, as believers in the paranormal, we would like to openly admit, there are a lot of faked paranormal photographs, videos, and other pieces of evidence out there. There are even in-depth debunking videos of certain television paranormal investigators. It is this kind of thing that has unfortunately dented the integrity of the paranormal investigative field and has caused the majority of the researchers, who are honest and true to their work, to be painted with the same brush as those that continue to put out fake evidence. It is because of this that there are so many people out there who are so quick in their decision making when it comes to declaring a piece of evidence as a fake. No matter how convinced you may be that the evidence is the best yet to be captured, and despite potentially looking at the most ground-breaking picture or video footage, they will simply dismiss it as another hoax, as they would have done with all of the previous evidence showed to them.

For this reason, I really struggle to hold out much hope for the future of paranormal evidence. The more complex and realistic computer programming becomes, the less believable paranormal evidence will be to the hard-nosed sceptic or even to the people sitting on the fence. It will become increasingly more difficult to convince people that the paranormal exists, despite potentially having some fantastic evidence at hand.

In my opinion, and as I have stated several times already, paranormal experiences are very personal, and this is where the future of paranormal investigating lies. Of course, as technology develops to hinder our progress in terms of proving our evidence to be true, it will also develop to allow us more ways of capturing evidence. The more equipment that we can develop that allows us to see outside of our limited range of perception, the better our chances will be of capturing the energies that reside there.

I truly believe that the investigative field has plateaued and become stale in many ways. It continues to use the same pieces of equipment. It continues to ask the same questions when seemingly interacting with spirits. It continues to, as a majority, assume that it is always dealing with a spirit that had once inhabited a living body. The field must progress in order to stay relevant, and this will be done by changing its viewpoint, by focusing on new ways of researching and by beginning to evolve from the old way of thinking to a new, more fluid way of thinking where there is an ability to accept, or at least consider, what may seem like outrageous theories that may go on to become fact.

Despite my slightly negative viewpoint on the paranormal investigative field, I do actually hold high hopes for its future. I am confident that with a fresh way of tackling the research and a new wave of investigators, we truly can take the research to the next level and begin to make believers out of the sceptics, and you can play a massive part in its rejuvenation.

Good luck, keep safe and have fun!

THE END

Special Thanks

I would like to thank all of the witnesses and experiencers who have allowed me to use their personal encounters for the purposes of this book. A special thank you to Kelly, Lee, and their family for allowing me to investigate their family home and use the footage captured there to form large parts of this book and my presentations. Without people like you the research field would cease to exist.

About Kieran Woodhouse

Kieran is an England based paranormal investigator, a public speaker on the subject and host of the Paranormal Paradigm Podcast and The Collective Conspiracy Show.

Kieran can be reached via his email address: kieran.woodhouse@gmail.com or via the podcast email address: paranormalparadigmpodcast@gmail.com.

Please feel free to contact him regarding any stories or information about the world of the paranormal or regarding any investigation enquiries.

Printed in Dunstable, United Kingdom

70467549R00070